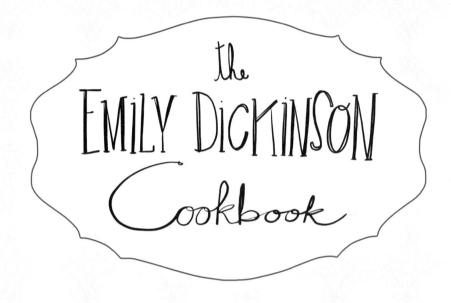

the
EMILY DICKINSON
Cookbook

Brimming with creative inspiration, how-to projects, and useful information to enrich your everyday life, Quarto Knows is a favorite destination for those pursuing their interests and passions. Visit our site and dig deeper with our books into your area of interest: Quarto Creates, Quarto Cooks, Quarto Homes, Quarto Lives, Quarto Drives, Quarto Explores, Quarto Gifts, or Quarto Kids.

© 2022 Quarto Publishing Group USA Inc.
Text © 2022 Aryln Osborne
Photography © 2022 Quarto Publishing Group USA Inc.

First Published in 2022 by The Harvard Common Press
an imprint of The Quarto Group,
100 Cummings Center, Suite 265-D,
Beverly, MA 01915, USA.
T (978) 282-9590 F (978) 283-2742 QuartoKnows.com

The Harvard Common Press titles are also available at discount for retail, wholesale, promotional, and bulk purchase. For details, contact the Special Sales Manager by email at specialsales@quarto.com or by mail at The Quarto Group, Attn: Special Sales Manager, 100 Cummings Center, Suite 265-D, Beverly, MA 01915, USA.

26 25 24 23 22   1 2 3 4 5

ISBN: 978-0-7603-7436-8

Digital edition published in 2022
eISBN: 978-0-7603-7437-5

Library of Congress Cataloging-in-Publication Data available

Design: Samantha J. Bednarek, samanthabednarek.com
Cover Illustration: Mara Penny/Lilla Rogers Studio
Page Layout: Samantha J. Bednarek, samanthabednarek.com
Recipe Photography: Michelle Miller
Archive Photography: Courtesy of Amherst College Digital Collections (ACDC)
Additional Photography: page 50 and 52 (top) Courtesy of the Emily Dickinson Museum; page 51 and 52 (bottom) Courtesy of Erik Gilg
Illustration: Mara Penny/Lilla Rogers Studio

Printed in China

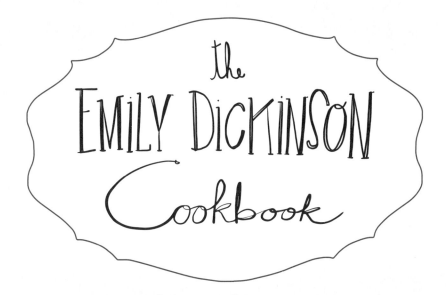

the EMILY DICKINSON Cookbook

RECIPES FROM EMILY'S TABLE ALONGSIDE THE POEMS THAT INSPIRE THEM

Arlyn Osborne

HARVARD COMMON PRESS

Contents

INTRODUCTION:
A Poet at Home in the Kitchen 6

Cinnamon Doughnuts, page 100

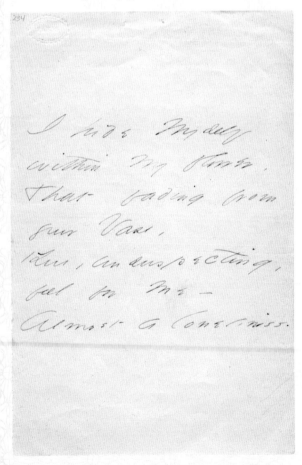

Vegetarian Niçoise Salad, page 59

Introduction
A POET AT HOME IN THE KITCHEN

EMILY DICKINSON is considered one of the greatest American poets today. But while she lived, Emily, a nineteenth-century rebel spinster, was known as an accomplished cook. This was her love language. She'd package a piece of cake or a recipe with her letters. Her father refused all bread but hers. And she was a competitive baker at the annual Amherst Cattle Show, where she took home second place for her Rye and Indian Loaf (page 72).

*Pumpkin
Corn Chowder*
page 47

Creme Puffs, page 96

Winter Garden Vegetable Soup, page 10

The kitchen was probably Emily's favorite room in the Dickinson Homestead. She spent hours inside its soft apple-green walls and baked regularly with Maggie, her cherished maid. The poet would often scribble on scraps of kitchen papers from shopping lists, to dinner invitations, to torn parchment. She once wrote a poem on the back of a French chocolate wrapper and wrote a recipe on the back of a poem. She used kitchen twine to bind her rhymes into booklets and was always happy to swipe a cookie when Maggie wasn't looking to sneak to children. The kitchen was where Emily felt most at home.

Food was an inspiration for the poet in all forms. Emily kept a watchful eye on the orchards and vegetable gardens and tended carefully to her beloved herbs.

Before becoming the notorious all-white-wearing recluse, Emily was a vivacious and witty woman, active in the community. She was part of a poetry club, a reading club, a sewing society, and a Shakespeare club. As she sunk deeper and deeper into the tide of agoraphobia, the poet held on to her love of cooking. She felt joy in the joy it gave others. With a rope, Emily would cautiously lower Cream Puffs (page 96) or a basket of Gingerbread (page 74) from her second-story window, hiding because she couldn't bear to be seen. She wasn't crazy. She was just an eccentric in need of some modern mental health awareness.

Emily mentioned food in many of her cryptic poems and often used hunger, starvation, and thirst as metaphors for emotional needs. The Belle of Amherst "had been hungry all the years."

This collection of fifty recipes is guided by a variety of components. First, Emily wrote some of her own recipes and those are adapted here for the modern cook. Some recipes are interpretations of foods mentioned in letters or inspired by her poems. Others highlight popular dishes in Victorian America that Emily would have likely eaten.

Just like the popular television series, *Dickinson*, I wanted to bridge the modern with the past. I did this not just by including modern equipment, but also by incorporating dishes popular today that Emily may not have necessarily see. Like Emily, I'm using food as a metaphor.

I also wanted to use the recipes as a way to tell Emily's story, because food, like poetry, was so incredibly meaningful to her. In many ways, food was her lifeline, an act of self-care and an expression of love, even in the depths of her seclusion. Despite everything we know about Emily, parts of her life will forever remain a mystery.

I hope the recipes in this book inspire you to be creative in the kitchen and to share it with those closest to you, just like Emily did.

Arlyn

CHAPTER 1

Breakfast
AND
Brunches

Baked Berry
Pecan French Toast
page 22

Egg-in-a-Basket with Chives

BREAKFAST was a special time for the Dickinson household. The tight-knit family ate the most important meal of the day together often and Maggie, the cook, knew everyone's favorites. In a letter to her cousins, Emily describes a "happy egg and toast" provided by Maggie.

Who can't help but smile when they see a plate of eggs-in-a-basket? It's one of the happiest egg and toast combinations out there. This classic version is prepared on the stovetop for a quick and easy breakfast that is sure to bring you joy.

1 slice sandwich bread
1 tablespoon (14 g) unsalted butter
1 egg
Kosher salt
Minced chives, for garnish

1. Stamp a hole out of the center of the bread slice using a biscuit or cookie cutter.

2. In a nonstick skillet, melt the butter over medium-low heat. Place the bread in the skillet and cook for 3 minutes, or until toasted. Turn over the bread. Crack the egg into the hole and season with salt. Cover with a lid and cook for 5 minutes, or until the egg is set. Garnish with chives before serving.

MAKES 1 SERVING

Spicy Skillet Hash

Will there really be a morning?
Is there such a thing as day?
Could I see it from the mountains
If I were as tall as they?

Has it feet like water-lilies?
Has it feathers like a bird?
Is it brought from famous countries
Of which I have never heard?

Oh, some scholar! Oh, some sailor!
Oh, some wise man from the skies!
Please to tell a little pilgrim
Where the place called morning lies!

A DISH THAT COULD BE FOUND at the Dickinsons' morning table was hash. In a letter to her brother, Emily wrote about all the breakfast foods laid across table, hash being one of them.

The term *hash* was adapted from the French word *hacher*, which means "to chop." A pan-fried dish of odds and ends, hash was a quick way to repurpose leftovers into a brand-new meal.

Almost anything can turn into a delicious hash, and it's a wonderful way to clean out the fridge. This recipe revives a mountain of leftover potatoes with bacon, peppers, and spices. It's the perfect meal to start the day.

---

6 slices bacon, diced
1 pound (455 g) leftover cooked
    potatoes, diced
1 small onion, diced
1 red bell pepper, cored and diced
1 jalapeño, diced
½ teaspoon paprika
½ teaspoon kosher salt
Hot sauce, for serving

1. In a large cast-iron skillet, cook the bacon over medium heat for about 10 minutes, or until crisp. Drain the bacon on paper towels. Set aside.

2. Increase the heat to medium-high. Stir the potatoes, onion, bell pepper, jalapeño, paprika, and salt into the bacon fat in the skillet and cook for 15 minutes, until tender and crispy.

3. Stir the bacon back into the skillet and cook until warm. Serve with hot sauce.

MAKES 4 SERVINGS

Sheet Pan Sausage Breakfast

Morning that comes but once,
Considers coming twice —
Two Dawns upon a single Morn,
Make Life a sudden price.

THE NINETEENTH century brought luxury to what was once an unexciting morning meal. Dining tables dazzled with never-before variety and larger servings of meat. Each region had its own specialty. Ham and grits in the South, chile peppers in the West, and dishes like French toast and eggs Benedict could be found in urban cities. As for the Northeast, sausages and hash browns were the key attraction. The dynamic "meat and potato" breakfast duo was a dish much enjoyed at the Dickinson Homestead.

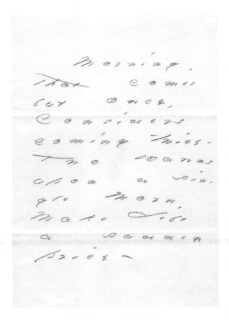

20 ounces (560 g) frozen shredded hash brown potatoes
4 tablespoons (56 g) unsalted butter, melted
½ teaspoon garlic powder
¼ teaspoon dried oregano
Kosher salt and black pepper
8 breakfast sausage links
4 eggs

1. Preheat the oven to 425°F (220°C, or gas mark 7).

2. Grease a rimmed baking sheet, add the hash browns, and drizzle with the melted butter. Sprinkle with the garlic powder, oregano, salt, and pepper. Toss to coat and scatter the sausages on top.

3. Bake for 30 minutes, or until the hash browns begin to turn golden.

4. Hollow out four wells in the hash browns and crack in the eggs. Bake for 10 minutes longer, or until the eggs are set.

MAKES 4 SERVINGS

Strawberry Oatmeal

Forbidden fruit a flavor has
That lawful orchards mocks;
How luscious lies the pea within
The pod that Duty locks!

FRUIT as a forbidden food was a regular theme in Emily's poetry. Emily hid hints about Sue Gilbert, her sister-in-law and neighbor, in her meters often and it's very probable that these off-limit fruits represented the poet's off-limit sweetheart. When ripe and in season, strawberries were a special treat for Emily. She tended them in the garden, received them as gifts, and wrote about them in her poems and letters.

This strawberry oatmeal is luckily within reach. It's sweet and tart, creamy and comforting, and scattered with fresh, juicy berries. Emily's father grew and sold oats from his wheat fields, but store-bought rolled oats will do just fine here.

3 cups (450 g) diced strawberries, divided
1 ½ cups (360 ml) water
2 cups (480 g) milk
2 cups (160 g) old-fashioned rolled oats
1 teaspoon vanilla extract
Pinch of kosher salt

1. Place 2 cups (300 g) of the diced strawberries in a blender and add the water. Blend until smooth.

2. Pour the strawberry mixture into a large saucepan and stir in the milk, oats, vanilla, and salt. Bring to a steady simmer. Cook for 10 minutes, or until thick and creamy, adjusting the heat as needed. Serve hot and garnish with the remaining diced strawberries.

MAKES 4 SERVINGS

Glazed Crullers

She sweeps with many-colored brooms,
And leaves the shreds behind;
Oh, housewife in the evening west,
Come back, and dust the pond!

You dropped a purple ravelling in,
You dropped an amber thread;
And now you've littered all the East
With duds of emerald!

And still she plies her spotted brooms,
And still the aprons fly,
Till brooms fade softly into stars —
And then I come away.

IN THE 1840S, Joseph Lyman visited the Dickinsons home for an extended stay. Emily's older brother Austin was delighted to host his friend and former classmate, who fell right in with the family and considered it a home away from home. Emily enjoyed the opportunity to practice her German and have clever conversations. On the other hand, Emily's younger sister, Lavinia, nicknamed Vinnie, was desperately and publicly in love with Joseph the entire time.

But for Mrs. Dickinson, this prolonged guest was a chance to show off her remarkable domestic expertise. And this did not go unnoticed. Joseph saw Mrs. Dickinson as a superior homemaker, praised her cooking, and claimed she had an extraordinary talent when it came to "crullers and custard." Joseph, who learned the fundamentals of housekeeping at the Homestead, later went on to write a manual on the topic.

In this poem, Emily compares a sunset to a housewife at work, sweeping and dusting, with her apron on. These charming crullers are truly a beautiful art. They're sweet, airy, and worthy of recognition.

(Continued)

1 cup (240 ml) water
½ cup (1 stick, or 112 g) unsalted butter, cut into pieces
1 cup (120 g) all-purpose flour
¼ teaspoon kosher salt
4 eggs
1 ½ cups (180 g) powdered sugar
3 tablespoons (45 ml) milk
½ teaspoon vanilla extract
Vegetable oil

1. Line a rimmed baking sheet with parchment paper.

2. In a large saucepan, bring the water and butter to a boil over medium-high heat. Take off the heat. Add the flour and salt and mix vigorously with a wooden spoon until well combined. Return to the stovetop. Cook over medium-high heat, stirring constantly, for 3 minutes, or until the dough forms into a ball.

3. Transfer the dough to a large bowl and allow to cool for 5 minutes. Beat in the eggs one at a time with an electric hand mixer. Continue to beat until thick and smooth. Add the dough to a pastry bag fitted with a large star tip.

4. Pipe twelve 2 ½-inch (6.5 cm) rings of dough onto the prepared baking sheet. Freeze for 15 minutes, or until stiff enough to lift by hand.

5. In a medium bowl, stir together the powdered sugar, milk, and vanilla; set aside.

6. In a large Dutch oven, heat 2 inches (5 cm) of oil to 350°F (180°C, or gas mark 4). Working in batches of three, carefully add the chilled dough to the oil and fry until golden on both sides. Drain on a wire rack set in a rimmed baking sheet. Dip one side of the crullers into the glaze while still warm and allow to set before serving.

MAKES 12 SERVINGS

Sticky Baked Peaches

Talk not to me of Summer Trees
The foliage of the mind
A Tabernacle is for Birds
Of no corporeal kind
And winds do go that way at noon
To their Ethereal Homes
Whose Bugles call the least of us
To undepicted Realms

EMILY, like any curious cook, enjoyed trying out new recipes and working with seasonal produce. On a warm May day, Emily wrote to her cousin: "I cooked the peaches as you told me, and they swelled to beautiful fleshy halves and tasted quite magic."

Summer delivers the finest peaches, best picked right from the trees. This recipe splits summer's stone jewel down the middle and bakes them until tender and caramelized. A drizzle of maple syrup and a scatter of granola (embraced in the nineteenth century) reinforces the sticky appeal and adds a satisfying crunch. It really does taste like magic. For a dessert version, swap out the yogurt for vanilla ice cream.

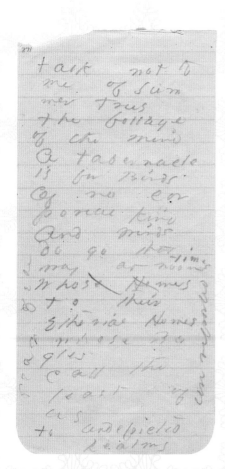

4 ripe peaches, halved and pitted
2 tablespoons (28 g) unsalted butter, melted
3 tablespoons (42 g) brown sugar
Greek yogurt, for serving
Granola, for serving

1. Preheat the oven to 375°F (190°C, gas mark 5). Grease a 9-inch (23 cm) square baking dish.

2. Place the halved peaches in the baking dish flesh-side up. Brush the peaches with the melted butter and sprinkle evenly with the brown sugar.

3. Bake for 20 minutes, or until tender. Serve warm with Greek yogurt and granola.

MAKES 4 SERVINGS

Baked Berry Pecan French Toast

The morns are meeker than they were,
The nuts are getting brown;
The berry's cheek is plumper,
The rose is out of town.

The maple wears a gayer scarf,
The field a scarlet gown.
Lest I should be old-fashioned,
I'll put a trinket on.

EMILY LOVED all the seasons, but she really had a soft spot for autumn. She wrote about it incessantly, not just in her poetry, but in her letters too. In this poem, Emily narrates the opening act of autumn. The busy energy of summer gives way to peaceful, quiet mornings. Roses fade as nuts and berries start to flourish. Nature, as if it were a person, changes its outfit from sunny green to brilliant shades of burgundy, gold, and russet. Emily, too, should consider keeping up with fashion.

This baked French toast is a celebration of autumn's most enchanting flavors and colors. Layers of buttery brioche are cooked in a creamy vanilla custard and topped with bright berries and toasted pecans. Finish it off with a stream of amber maple syrup.

1 pound (455 g) dry brioche bread, cubed
8 eggs
2 cups (480 ml) milk
½ cup (120 g) heavy cream
½ cup (110 g) packed brown sugar
1 tablespoon (15 ml) vanilla extract
1 teaspoon ground cinnamon
¼ teaspoon kosher salt
1 cup (150 g) mixed berries, such as raspberries, blackberries, and blueberries
½ cup (70 g) pecans, chopped
Powdered sugar, for garnish

1. Preheat the oven to 350°F (180°C, or gas mark 4). Grease a 13 x 9-inch (33 x 23 cm) baking pan.

2. Spread the dry bread cubes evenly in the prepared pan.

3. In a large bowl, whisk together the eggs, milk, heavy cream, brown sugar, vanilla, cinnamon, and salt. Pour the mixture over the bread, mix gently, and allow to soak for 10 minutes. Sprinkle with the berries and pecans.

4. Bake for 45 minutes, or until the bread is puffed and golden. Cool slightly. Dust with powdered sugar before serving.

MAKES 8 SERVINGS

Apple Pancakes

A drop fell on the apple tree,
Another on the roof;
A half a dozen kissed the eaves,
And made the gables laugh.

A few went out to help the brook,
That went to help the sea.
Myself conjectured, Were they pearls,
What necklaces could be!

The dust replaced in hoisted roads,
The birds jocoser sung;
The sunshine threw his hat away,
The orchards spangles hung.

The breezes brought dejected lutes,
And bathed them in the glee;
The East put out a single flag,
And signed the fete away.

A LOT WAS HAPPENING at the breakfast table in the nineteenth century. For the first time ever there were options when it came to the morning menu.

A plush apple orchard sat on the Dickinson property and it delivered every year. It was of great inspiration to Emily, who wrote often of orchards, apples, and even cider. In a letter to Austin, she scribed: "Our apples are ripening fast. I am fully convinced that with your approbation they will not only pick themselves, but arrange one another in baskets and present themselves to be eaten."

This poem details the progression of a rainstorm. It begins slow, with just a drop on the apple tree. Slowly but surely, nature is bathed in rain.

These pancakes, laced with shredded apples, are best dished out by the stack, hot, buttered, and dripping with syrup. They're perfect for any morning, rain or shine.

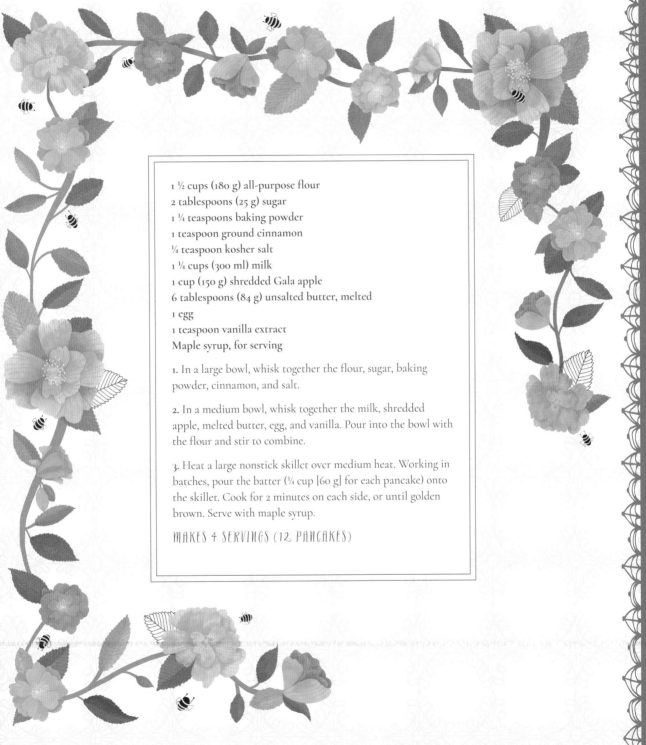

1 ½ cups (180 g) all-purpose flour
2 tablespoons (25 g) sugar
1 ¼ teaspoons baking powder
1 teaspoon ground cinnamon
¼ teaspoon kosher salt
1 ¼ cups (300 ml) milk
1 cup (150 g) shredded Gala apple
6 tablespoons (84 g) unsalted butter, melted
1 egg
1 teaspoon vanilla extract
Maple syrup, for serving

1. In a large bowl, whisk together the flour, sugar, baking powder, cinnamon, and salt.

2. In a medium bowl, whisk together the milk, shredded apple, melted butter, egg, and vanilla. Pour into the bowl with the flour and stir to combine.

3. Heat a large nonstick skillet over medium heat. Working in batches, pour the batter (¼ cup [60 g] for each pancake) onto the skillet. Cook for 2 minutes on each side, or until golden brown. Serve with maple syrup.

MAKES 4 SERVINGS (12 PANCAKES)

CHAPTER 2

Teatime
AT THE
Dickinson's

Cherry Scones
page 37

Jasmine Tea Biscuits

Come slowly, Eden!
Lips unused to thee,
Bashful, sip thy jasmines,
As the fainting bee,

Reaching late his flower,
Round her chamber hums,
Counts his nectars — enters,
And is lost in balms!

A GREAT SOURCE of pain came from Emily's attempt at inserting herself into the convoluted life of heartthrob Samuel Bowles. She was sick in love with him and never stopped. When he wasn't near, she loved him from afar. The possible recipient of the mysterious Master Letters (a series of three desperate love notes written to someone Emily calls "Master" but doesn't identify) received some of Emily's best work, but didn't really care.

Victorians attached symbolic meaning to plants and more than a third of Emily's poems include flowers. The editor of the *Springfield Republican* called Emily his "Daisy," an affectionate nickname, and gifted her a jasmine vine, which to Emily implied he was her soul mate. Emily treasured and tended the precious vine for decades.

These buttery shortbread cookies bloom with the bright floral flavor of jasmine tea. Enjoy them with someone special.

½ cup (1 stick, or 112 g) unsalted butter, softened
¼ cup (30 g) powdered sugar
1 tablespoon (5 g) jasmine tea leaves, finely chopped
1 cup (120 g) all-purpose flour
¼ teaspoon kosher salt

1. In a large bowl, beat the butter, powdered sugar, jasmine tea, and salt with an electric hand mixer until fluffy. Add the flour and salt and beat on low speed just until combined.

2. Lay a sheet of plastic wrap on your work surface and place the cookie dough in the center. Shape the dough into a 9-inch (23 cm) log and roll up securely in the plastic. Refrigerate for a minimum of 1 hour.

3. Preheat the oven to 350°F (180°C, or gas mark 4). Line a cookie sheet with parchment paper.

4. Cut the dough into ¼-inch (6 mm) rounds and arrange on the prepared cookie sheet. Bake for 13 minutes, or until the cookies are lightly golden around the edges. Allow to cool for 5 minutes on the cookie sheet. Remove the cookies to a wire rack and cool completely.

MAKES ABOUT 3 DOZEN COOKIES

Rice Cakes

The grave my little cottage is,
Where, keeping house for thee,
I make my parlor orderly,
And lay the marble tea,

For two divided, briefly,
A cycle, it may be,
Till everlasting life unite
In strong society.

BEFORE MARRYING Emily's brother, Susan Gilbert left Amherst to teach in Baltimore. Emily missed Sue dearly during their brief separation and wrote her countless letters. In one of her dispatches, the poet included a tasty rice cake. This was a teatime favorite in Victorian America and a special treat in the Dickinson household.

Rice flour was prized for its fine and light texture and was mainstream in New England by the mid-nineteenth century.

When making these rice cakes, make sure you use regular rice flour (not glutinous). These sweet buttery cakes are perfect with a warm pot of tea on any afternoon.

1 cup (120 g) rice flour
¼ teaspoon baking soda
¼ teaspoon kosher salt
½ cup (1 stick, or 112 g) unsalted butter, softened
1 cup (120 g) powdered sugar
2 eggs
2 tablespoons (30 ml) milk
2 teaspoons (10 ml) vanilla extract
Zest of 1 lemon

1. Preheat the oven to 350°F (180°C, or gas mark 4). Grease an 8-inch (20 cm) square cake pan and cover the bottom with parchment paper.

2. In a medium bowl, whisk together the rice flour, baking soda, and salt.

3. In a large bowl, beat the butter and powdered sugar with an electric hand mixer until fluffy. Beat in the eggs, milk, vanilla, and lemon zest. Add the flour mixture and beat on low speed just until combined. Pour the batter into the prepared pan.

4. Bake for about 18 minutes, or until a wooden toothpick inserted in the center of the cake comes out clean. Cool in the pan for 10 minutes, then unmold and allow the cake to cool on a wire rack. Slice into 16 squares and serve.

MAKES 16 SERVINGS

Honey Lemonade

The pedigree of honey
Does not concern the bee;
A clover, any time, to him
Is aristocracy.

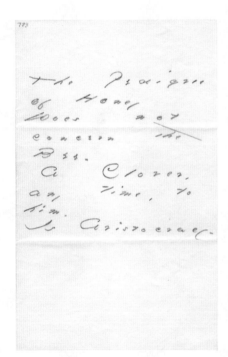

IN THIS POEM, Emily compares human values with those of nature. A special flower is not important to a bee, who can survive on the honey of any flower. To the bee, it's all the same, all noble. Even the average abundant clover.

Emily was a member of a Shakespeare club where "there were many little dances, with cake and lemonade at the end." Emily lived in a period hypnotized by the topic of Shakespeare. It was a universal part of American culture and everyone reveled in discussion and debate of the Bard. Shakespeare clubs existed all over the Northeast, and Amherst's budding poet found herself in one too. Emily refused to censor any of the passages. She was a true lover of words and wanted to read everything. Nothing was taboo. If someone started to cross out questionable texts, Emily would shut it down.

If you're cooling off with friends, a pitcher of this refreshing honey-sweetened lemonade will definitely create some buzz.

---

1 cup (340 g) honey
3 cups (720 ml) cold water, divided
1 cup (240 ml) lemon juice
Ice, for serving

1. In a small saucepan, heat the honey and 1 cup (240 ml) water over low heat until warm and fluid. Take off the heat.

2. In a serving pitcher, stir together the remaining 2 cups (480 ml) water, lemon juice, and honey syrup. Serve in glasses over ice.

MAKES 6 SERVINGS

Ham and Cucumber Tea Sandwiches

You asked the company to tea,
Acquaintance, just a few,
And chatted close with this grand thing
That don't remember you?

"OH, I WILL SEE YOU again at the Dickinson tea party," could be heard often during Commencement Week in nineteenth-century Amherst. Mr. and Mrs. Dickinson were a power couple in Amherst society, famous for their hospitality. Edward, a civic-minded man, served as the treasurer of Amherst College for almost forty years. During each year of his term, the Dickinsons hosted a grand Commencement Week tea party, where the Homestead flooded with elite company. Friends and acquaintances would chatter away, smiling, as they nibbled on elegant fare.

Teatime in the nineteenth century was a beloved ritual for the upper class. And Emily belonged to this world of costume dress-up and delicate food.

These sandwiches—made with salty ham, tangy cream cheese, and crisp cucumber—will fit in at any sophisticated function.

8 slices white or whole-wheat sandwich bread
½ cup (120 g) chive and onion–flavored cream cheese, softened
1 English cucumber, thinly sliced
8 deli slices Black Forest ham

1. Spread two slices of bread with 1 tablespoon (15 g) of cream cheese each.

2. Cover one of the slices with cucumber and top with 2 slices of ham. Top with the other slice of bread.

3. Make two diagonal cuts to create four triangular tea sandwiches. Repeat the process with the remaining ingredients.

MAKES 4 SERVINGS

Raspberry Jam

She rose to his requirement, dropped
The playthings of her life
To take the honorable work
Of woman and of wife.

If aught she missed in her new day
Of amplitude, or awe,
Or first prospective, or the gold
In using wore away,

It lay unmentioned, as the sea
Develops pearl and weed,
But only to himself is known
The fathoms they abide.

SUGAR WORK in early America was deemed an extraordinary talent, and so the art of making fruit spreads fell to the house mistress. At this point, sugar was a rare resource reserved for the rich, and this prestige placed jam on the tables of formal teas. In the nineteenth century, canning techniques were upgraded and sugar and fruit became less expensive and more available. These added benefits raised the pressure for housewives to produce crystal-clear jellies and robustly flavored jams. Reputation was at stake.

Emily might have been describing her own mother in this poem about a hardworking wife. Mrs. Dickinson certainly put her family before herself and exceeded what was required of her. If Mrs. Dickinson ever made jam, we can be sure it was done with great attention and finesse.

In this stress-free recipe, fresh raspberries are transformed into a vibrant, flavorful jam, worthy of a place at your tea table.

---

1 ½ pounds (672 g) fresh raspberries
5 cups (1 kg) sugar
Juice of 1 lemon
¾ cup (180 ml) water
One 1.75-ounce (50 g) package fruit pectin

1. In a medium saucepan, add the raspberries and crush with a wooden spoon. Stir in the sugar and lemon juice and allow to sit at room temperature for 15 minutes.

2. Stir in the water and pectin and transfer to the stovetop. Bring the mixture to a boil and cook, stirring regularly, for 3 minutes, or until the mixture has thickened slightly. Take off the heat and allow to cool completely.

MAKES 6 SERVINGS

Cherry Scones

"I wish you could have some cherries – if there was any way we would send you a basket of them – they are very large and delicious, and are just ripening now."
—Emily (1851)

EMILY'S WORK was incredibly visual. She was clearly inspired by her surroundings, which, if we're being honest, were not unfortunate. The Dickinson Homestead was a sparkling, colorful Eden, lush with gardens and groves. Emily had the best room in the house with a view of the meadow her family owned from her second-story window, right in front of her desk.

The family's fertile grounds produced magnificent cherries every year, which the poet watched over lovingly. She wrote to her brother: "Today is very beautiful – just as bright, just as blue, just as green and as white and as crimson as the cherry trees full in bloom." Emily was captivated.

These fluffy scones are studded with ruby cherries for a vibrant pop of color and a subtle bite of tanginess.

2 cups (240 g) all-purpose flour
3 tablespoons (38 g) sugar
1 tablespoon (8 g) baking powder
¼ teaspoon kosher salt
4 tablespoons (56 g) cold butter, cut into small pieces
1 cup (240 ml) cold heavy cream
½ cup (75 g) dried cherries
1 teaspoon vanilla extract

1. Preheat the oven to 425°F (220°C, or gas mark 7). Line a rimmed baking sheet with parchment paper.

2. In large bowl, stir together the flour, sugar, baking powder, and salt. Cut in the butter with a pastry blender.

3. Stir in the heavy cream, dried cherries, and vanilla just until combined.

4. Turn out the dough onto a floured work surface and shape into a 9-inch (23 cm) circle. Cut the dough into 8 wedges. Arrange the wedges on the prepared baking sheet.

5. Bake for 15 minutes, or until golden. Serve warm.

MAKES 8 SCONES

CHAPTER 3

From THE Stockpot

Pumpkin
Corn Chowder
page 47

Winter Garden Vegetable Soup

A little Snow was here and there
Disseminated in her Hair —
Since she and I had met and played
Decade had gathered to Decade —

But Time had added not obtained
Impregnable the Rose
For summer too indelible
Too obdurate for Snows —

107

A little Snow
was here and there
disseminated in her
Hair —
Since she and I
had met and played
Decade had hastened
to Decade — (hurried
gathered

But Time had added
not obtained inviolate —
innincible
Impregnable The Rose
for summer too
indelible ○ inscrutable
Too + obdurate — Our
Snows — Complent —

inviolate
+ illustrious the Rose —
+ sumptuous — Our Snows —
Impregnable The Rose
for Summer too inscrutable
Too sumptuous Our snows —

(Continued)

IN 1855, Edward upgraded the Dickinson Homestead with a kitchen renovation, a breezy veranda, and a fancy rooftop cupola. For Emily, bribed his favorite daughter with the installation of a winter conservatory. When sunny weather turned cold and the ground was covered with frost, Emily could still tend to her garden and flowers.

This poem is about snow, but also about how time passes between two friends. The appearance of Emily's companion has changed, her hair is gray. Yet she hasn't allowed the harshness of winter, which comes every year, to command her. Instead, she ages with grace and endurance and continues to bloom.

This charming winter vegetable soup is a recipe to keep for years and years. Warm and soothing, it's just the thing for a frosty day.

2 tablespoons (30 ml) olive oil, divided
1 pound (455 g) chicken sausage, sliced
2 small carrots, sliced
2 ribs celery, sliced
1 large leek (white part only), sliced
2 cloves garlic, minced
Kosher salt and black pepper
8 ounces (227 g) russet potato, peeled and
    cut into small cubes
8 ounces (227 g) butternut squash, peeled and
    cut into small cubes
1 quart (960 ml) chicken broth
1 cup (240 ml) water
One 15-ounce (420 g) can white beans, rinsed and drained
1 cup (30 g) shredded kale

1. In a large pot, heat 1 tablespoon (15 ml) of the olive oil over medium heat. Add the sausage and cook for 3 minutes, or until browned. Transfer the sausage to a plate; set aside.

2. Heat the remaining 1 tablespoon (15 ml) olive oil. Stir in the carrots, celery, leek, and garlic. Cook for 5 minutes, or until softened. Season with salt and pepper.

3. Stir in the potato, squash, chicken broth, and water. Bring to a boil. Lower the heat, cover, and simmer for 15 minutes, or until the vegetables are tender.

4. Return the chicken sausage to the pot and stir in the white beans and kale. Cook until heated through and the kale is wilted.

MAKES 6 SERVINGS

Beef Bone Broth

There's something quieter than sleep
Within this inner room!
It wears a sprig upon its breast,
And will not tell its name.

Some touch it and some kiss it,
Some chafe its idle hand;
It has a simple gravity
I do not understand!

While simple-hearted neighbors
Chat of the 'early dead,'
We, prone to periphrasis,
Remark that birds have fled!

DEATHBED SETTINGS were of great interest to Emily, who often pressed witnesses for specifics. Emily's mother, who had been suffering from a very serious cold, sipped beef broth in the final moments of her life. Mrs. Dickinson, although a very attentive mother, hadn't been very close to her daughters while they were growing up. Having to watch her mother suffer changed Emily and brought the two closer together. In this poem, Emily parallels a dying person to a bird that has fled. When Mrs. Dickinson finally passed, the poet wrote that her mother had "flown."

During the Victorian era, beef tea was ranked highly as a healing beverage. It was even given to Civil War soldiers as a form of treatment. The curative concoction lives on today under the name bone broth, which took over the nation with its appeal of rich nutrients and endless health benefits.

---

3 pounds (1365 g) beef bones
2 carrots, cut into chunks
2 ribs celery, cut into chunks
1 onion, cut into chunks
4 cloves garlic
10 cups (2400 ml) water
2 tablespoons (30 ml) white vinegar
1 bay leaf
1 teaspoon peppercorns

1. Preheat the oven to 450°F (230°C, or gas mark 8).

2. Arrange the beef bones on a rimmed baking sheet. Roast, turning halfway, for 30 minutes, or until well browned.

3. To a 6-quart (5.4 L) slow cooker, carefully add the beef bones and any juices. Stir in the carrots, celery, onion, garlic, water, vinegar, bay leaf, and peppercorns. Cover and cook on the lowest setting for 12 hours.

4. Line a large colander with several layers of cheesecloth and set over a large bowl. Strain the bone broth over the prepared colander. Serve immediately. Alternatively, allow to cool to room temperature and store in the refrigerator in airtight containers.

MAKES 8 SERVINGS

Brothy Chicken Soup

SUE, fell ill over the summer of 1854. When the worst was over, Emily took to her pen and paper to update her brother Austin on their shared beloved's recovery. The poet was very happy to report that the patient "had eaten chicken broth twice" that day.

Broth has been a prominent pillar of restorative cooking for centuries, regarded as a healing food for the sick. In American cooking, chicken soup is an age-old folk remedy that is still followed today. This warm brothy soup, made with tender vegetables and gentle herbs, is certain to comfort any ailment, big or small.

2 quarts (1.9 L) chicken broth
1 cup (240 ml) water
1 pound (455 g) boneless, skinless chicken breast
2 carrots, peeled and sliced
2 ribs celery, sliced
1 small onion, diced
Kosher salt and black pepper
3 tablespoons (6 g) chopped parsley

1. In a large pot, bring the chicken broth and water to a boil. Add the chicken breast. Lower the heat, cover, and simmer for 20 minutes, or until the chicken is fully cooked. Remove the chicken to a cutting board, allow to cool, and shred into pieces; set aside.

2. Stir the carrots, celery, and onion into the broth in the pot. Simmer for 20 minutes, or until the vegetables are tender. Return the shredded chicken to the pot and cook until heated through. Season with salt and pepper. Stir in the parsley.

MAKES 4 SERVINGS

Sue's Oyster Stew

We outgrow love like other things
And put it in the drawer,
Till it an antique fashion shows
Like costumes grandsires wore.

AFTER SUE MARRIED Austin, Emily was a regular guest at their home, the Evergreens, which Edward built for Austin and Sue on the Homestead property. The participants of this complicated love triangle were content. But Sue's ambitions ultimately got the best of her and her inner circle found her character more and more draining. Eventually, Emily and Sue (just like Austin and Sue) outgrew one another.

Sue went on to become sophisticated and worldly, recognized far and wide for her famous salon. She was in constant need of society, always throwing expensive parties where she was known to serve oyster stew as late as 10 p.m.

As fancy as it sounds, making oyster stew is really simple. There's no chopping and no shucking and it's ready in less than half an hour. Even still, there's no denying that this smoky, creamy delicacy really is luxurious.

1 pound (455 g) jarred shucked
   oysters, with juices
6 tablespoons (84 g) unsalted butter,
   cut into pieces
5 cups (1200 ml) half-and-half
1 teaspoon seafood seasoning
¼ teaspoon smoked paprika
Crackers, for serving

1. In a large pot, stir together the oysters, butter, half-and-half, seafood seasoning, and smoked paprika. Bring to a steady simmer over medium-high heat. Do not boil.

2. Adjust the heat and gently simmer for 12 minutes, or until the oysters are cooked through and the stew is hot. Serve with crackers.

MAKES 6 SERVINGS

Pumpkin Corn Chowder

'Twas just this time, last year, I died.
I know I heard the Corn,
When I was carried by the Farms—
It had the Tassels on—

I thought how yellow it would look—
When Richard went to mill—
And then, I wanted to get out,
But something held my will.

I thought just how Red—Apples wedged
The Stubble's joints between—
And the Carts went stooping round the fields
To take the Pumpkins in—

I wondered which would miss me, least,
And when Thanksgiving, came,
If Father'd multiply the plates—
To make an even Sum—

And would it blur the Christmas glee
My Stocking hang too high
For any Santa Claus to reach
The altitude of me—

But this sort, grieved myself,
And so, I thought the other way,
How just this time, some perfect year—
Themself, should come to me —

THIS POEM CELEBRATES THE BEAUTY of autumn and death, two of Emily's favorite subjects. The narrator is a young girl, dead for one year. She wasn't ready to leave her family and didn't want to miss out on the stunning splendor of autumn's brilliant harvest. Her coffin was carried across the farms when the corn was ripe and she wondered, like all of us do, how her family would go on without her. These thoughts made her sad, but she was uplifted by the idea of them rejoining her one day.

The best of fall's bounty exists in this recipe. Ripe yellow corn, glowing red apples, and creamy pumpkin cooked down into a sweet and savory chowder that celebrates autumn.

---

4 tablespoons (56 g) unsalted butter
1 small Braeburn apple, peeled and diced
1 small onion, diced
One 15-ounce (420 g) can pumpkin puree
One 10-ounce (280 g) package frozen sweet
    kernel corn, thawed
2 cups (480 ml) vegetable broth
2 cups (480 ml) half-and-half
¼ teaspoon nutmeg
Kosher salt

1. In a large pot, melt the butter over medium heat. Stir in the apple and onion and cook for 7 minutes, or until softened.

2. Stir in the pumpkin, corn, vegetable broth, half-and-half, and nutmeg. Adjust the heat and simmer gently for 10 minutes, or until heated through. Season with salt.

MAKES 4 SERVINGS

Irish Stew

"Maggie is making a flying visit to cattle-show, on her very robust wings—for Maggie is getting corpulent."
—*Emily (1881)*

EMILY AND MAGGIE, mistress and maid, were quite the pair. The two had an unquestionable and unique bond. Maggie, an Irish immigrant who had originally planned to trek out to California, remained a part of the Dickinson family for thirty years. The Dickinson Homestead employed numerous Irish American immigrants across the family estate. When Emily died, she had arranged for six Homestead staff members, all Irishmen, to carry her coffin. During Emily's life, she and Maggie spent a lot of time in the kitchen, baking, and cooking, and talking.

A hearty Irish stew might have been something Maggie made for the Dickinson family. Chunks of beef, potatoes, and carrots are simmered until fork-tender in a brew of flavorful broth and Irish stout. It's a hearty dish that feeds a crowd.

2 pounds (910 g) beef stew meat, cut into 1-inch (2.5 cm) cubes
Kosher salt and black pepper
2 tablespoons (30 ml) olive oil
1 onion, cut into chunks
2 cloves garlic, chopped
¼ cup (30 g) all-purpose flour
3 russet potatoes, peeled and cut into 1-inch (2.5 cm) pieces
2 carrots, cut into 1-inch (2.5 cm) pieces
1 quart (960 ml) beef broth
One 16-ounce (480 ml) bottle Guinness beer
1 teaspoon dried thyme

1. Season the beef with salt and pepper.

2. In a Dutch oven, heat the oil over medium-high heat. Add half of the beef to the hot oil and cook for 5 minutes, or until well browned. Transfer the beef to a plate and repeat with the remaining beef.

3. Lower the heat to medium and add the onion. Cook for 5 minutes, or until softened. Add the garlic and stir until fragrant, about 10 seconds. Return the beef back to the pot. Sprinkle with the flour and stir to coat.

4. Stir in the potatoes, carrots, beef broth, beer, and thyme. Bring to a boil. Lower the heat, cover, and simmer for 30 minutes, or until the beef and vegetables are tender.

MAKES 6 SERVINGS

If it weren't for Mabel Todd, Austin's longstanding lover, much of Emily's work would have never been published. Austin and Mabel were very calculated in their encounters and used the Dickinson dining room as a safe meeting place. After Emily's death, Mabel teamed up with the poet's long-term correspondent, Thomas Wentworth Higginson. Together they published many of Emily's poems.

A recurring guest in the Dickinson dining room was Benjamin Newton, who regularly joined the family for dinner while he worked as a law apprentice for Edward. Emily described Newton (that's what she called him) as one of her earliest friends. The poet was a student at Mount Holyoke when she returned home to fight off a fierce cold. Over the next several weeks, Emily and Newton discovered their shared passion for books and clicked instantly.

Emily may have inherited her love of cooking from her mother, who likely gave her some pointers in the kitchen. The two were very similar. Both enjoyed gardening, participated in the Cattle Show, and fell under spells of melancholy. Emily, however, was not a fan of cleaning and thought housekeeping was "a prickly art."

Of the three Dickinson children, Emily and Austin were the closest. They had the same sense of humor, valued solitude over society, and stood up to their overbearing father. The siblings were often each other's built-in amusement at the dining table and spent many nights talking by the kitchen hearth when the rest of the house was asleep.

Emily's family dining room was no stranger to the elite. Many political figures, professors, editors, and beautiful people once walked the rooms of the Homestead, drink in hand. The poet belonged to one of the most prominent families in Amherst and her parents were well known for their generous hospitality.

Emily's father, Edward, was a hot-tempered tyrant who smothered his family with his rules and expectations. Austin and Emily shared an inside joke referring to the Homestead as "head-quarters." Maybe it was after dinner or while Emily was setting the table, but when Edward complained about a chipped piece of tableware, Emily walked out of the house and shattered it on the ground.

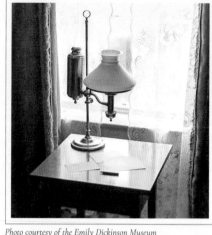

Photo courtesy of the Emily Dickinson Museum

When Mr. and Mrs. Dickinson left town for a weekend trip, Emily and Austin eagerly decided to throw a house party. They invited all their friends, moved the rug for dancing, and set out refreshments. When their parents returned, Mrs. Dickinson noticed the rug was upside down. She wasn't happy about the party, but chose not to tell her husband.

95-13

Are Friends
Delight or Pain?
Could Bounty
but remain
Riches were good.

But if they
only last
+ Compose
Ill cannot
Riches are sad.

+ Bolder.

I cannot want
it more –
I cannot want
it less –
My Human Nature's
fullest force
Expends itself
on this.

And still it
is nothing
to him who
easily wins – itself
is worth
or distance
his fathoms are
certain.

To lash the
Magic Creature
till it fell,
yet that Whiss
name
too noble then
to tell.

Magnanimous
Bird
to do deserved
Singing unto the
Stone
Of which it died.

Shame need not
crouch
In such an
Earth as Ours –
Shame – Stand erect
The universe is yours.

95-10

"Was Box"
was all the
Statement.
The Apprehension
vitas –
Perhaps – the
Comprehension.
they more
one Lexicons.

But les X
for Speculation

CHAPTER 4

Poetic Suppers

Pan-Fried
Cod Cakes
page 69

Lemon Herb Chicken

Before I got my eye put out,
I liked as well to see
As other creatures that have eyes,
And know no other way.

But were it told to me, to-day,
That I might have the sky
For mine, I tell you that my heart
Would split, for size of me.

The meadows mine, the mountains mine, —
All forests, stintless stars,
As much of noon as I could take
Between my finite eyes.

The motions of the dipping birds,
The lightning's jointed road,
For mine to look at when I liked, —
The news would strike me dead!

So safer, guess, with just my soul
Upon the window-pane
Where other creatures put their eyes,
Incautious of the sun.

IN THIS POEM, Emily illustrates seeing the world in two versions. At first, she sees what everyone else sees. But once the sun took out her eyes, she was able to see more splendor than ever before. She realizes that this beauty is so intense and so powerful, that it would kill her to see it again. It's much safer to view the world as everyone else does, with a windowpane in between.

When Emily was in her thirties, she suffered from an eye disorder that caused her to spend eight months in Boston for treatments. When she finally returned home, she couldn't do much except housework. She wrote: "For the first few weeks I did nothing but comfort my plants . . . I chop the chicken centres when we have roast fowl."

This roast chicken is flavored with fresh green herbs and glimmering lemon. Like the sun, it's bright and beautiful.

---

4 tablespoons (56 g) unsalted butter, melted
Juice of 1 lemon
1 ½ teaspoons Italian seasoning
½ teaspoon kosher salt
½ teaspoon garlic powder
⅛ teaspoon black pepper
4 boneless, skinless chicken breasts
Chopped parsley, for garnish
Lemon, sliced, for serving

1. Preheat the oven to 375°F (190°C, gas mark 5).

2. In a small bowl, stir together the melted butter, lemon juice, Italian seasoning, salt, garlic powder, and pepper.

3. Arrange the chicken in a 13 x 9-inch (33 x 23 cm) baking dish. Pour the butter mixture over the chicken and turn to coat.

4. Bake for 20 minutes, or until the chicken is cooked through. Arrange the chicken on a serving platter and drizzle with the pan juices. Sprinkle with chopped parsley and serve with sliced lemons.

MAKES 4 SERVINGS

Vegetarian Niçoise Salad

"The garden is amazing – we have beets and beans, splendid potatoes."
—*Emily (1852)*

THE DICKINSON Homestead flourished with grain meadows, vegetable plots, and fruit trees. Chickens, among other farm animals, were also kept on the property. Emily enjoyed watching the produce grow and change with the seasons and was very moved by it.

This vibrant salad, bursting with color and texture, is a wonderful way to showcase all the ingredients that would have been found at Emily's family home.

12 ounces (340 g) small yellow potatoes
8 ounces (227 g) green beans, trimmed
4 cups (120 g) baby arugula
4 hard-boiled eggs, quartered
1 cup (100 g) quartered radishes
1 cup (110 g) sliced cucumber
1 cup (150 g) halved cherry tomatoes
1 cup (120 g) shredded beets
½ cup (75 g) pitted Kalamata olives
Balsamic dressing, for serving
Kosher salt and black pepper

1. In a large pot, add the potatoes and enough water to cover. Bring to a boil. Lower the heat and simmer for 15 minutes, or until tender. Drain and allow to cool slightly. Slice the potatoes in half; set aside.

2. Fill a large bowl with ice water. Rinse the pot used for the potatoes and fill halfway with water. Bring to a boil, then add the green beans. Cook for 3 minutes, or until vibrant. Drain the green beans and submerge in the prepared ice water. Drain on paper towels; set aside.

3. Place the arugula in a large serving platter or bowl. On top of the arugula, arrange the potatoes, green beans, eggs, radishes, cucumber, tomatoes, beets, and olives. Drizzle with dressing and season with salt and pepper.

MAKES 4 TO 6 SERVINGS

Veal Meatballs with Gravy

Some keep the Sabbath going to church;
I keep it staying at home,
With a bobolink for a chorister,
And an orchard for a dome.

Some keep the Sabbath in surplice;
I just wear my wings,
And instead of tolling the bell for church,
Our little sexton sings.

God preaches, — a noted clergyman, —
And the sermon is never long;
So instead of getting to heaven at last,
I'm going all along!

WHEN EMILY WAS SIXTEEN, she attended Mount Holyoke Female Seminary, only 10 miles away in South Hadley, Massachusetts. The curriculum was rigorous, covering botany, astronomy, philosophy, history, and music. Physical exercise was encouraged and participation in domestic duties were mandatory. Emily washed, dried, and set out the knives for every table at mealtime.

Mount Holyoke, like many academic institutions of the era, prioritized religion and applauded their ability to restore undecided pupils to God. But Emily had her doubts, never gave in to the faith, and therefore was labeled hopeless. In this poem, Emily expresses her feelings toward religion. The poet prefers to worship nature.

While Emily was at school, she took a break from her rebellion to gush over a mouthwatering menu. She sent her brother a bill of fare that included veal and gravy and wrote a note that said: "Isn't that a dinner fit to set before a King."

This recipe turns ground veal into juicy, flavorful meatballs that are coated in a rich gravy. It's a dinner worth a royal audience, or at the very least, writing about.

VEAL MEATBALLS

1 egg
½ cup (50 g) Italian breadcrumbs
¼ cup (15 g) chopped parsley
2 cloves garlic, minced
1 ¼ teaspoons kosher salt
⅛ teaspoon pepper
1 pound (454 g) ground veal

GRAVY

1 tablespoon (14 g) unsalted butter
1 onion, thinly sliced
1 tablespoon (8 g) all-purpose flour
1 ½ cups (360 ml) beef broth
2 teaspoons (10 ml) Worcestershire sauce

Cooked egg noodles, for serving

1. Preheat the oven broiler. Grease a rimmed baking sheet.

2. To make the meatballs, in a large bowl, stir together the egg, breadcrumbs, parsley, garlic, salt, and pepper. Mix in the ground veal. Form into 1-tablespoon (15 g) meatballs and arrange on the prepared baking sheet. Broil for 8 minutes, or until cooked through.

3. To make the gravy, in a large nonstick skillet, melt the butter over medium heat. Add the onion and cook for 5 minutes, or until soft and lightly golden. Stir in the flour and cook for 1 minute. Stir in the beef broth and Worcestershire sauce. Bring to a boil, then lower the heat and simmer for 3 to 5 minutes, or until thickened.

4. Stir the cooked meatballs into the gravy to coat. Serve with egg noodles.

MAKES 4 SERVINGS

Mushroom Pot Pie

The mushroom is the elf of plants,
At evening it is not;
At morning in a truffled hut
It stops upon a spot

As if it tarried always;
And yet its whole career
Is shorter than a snake's delay,
And fleeter than a tare.

'Tis vegetation's juggler,
The germ of alibi;
Doth like a bubble antedate,
And like a bubble hie.

I feel as if the grass were pleased
To have it intermit;
The surreptitious scion
Of summer's circumspect.

Had nature any outcast face,
Could she a son contemn,
Had nature an Iscariot,
That mushroom, -- it is him.

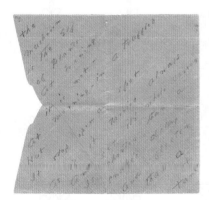

EMILY CALLS THE MUSHROOM the elf of plants. This elf, the mushroom, is always loitering and the grass is happy when he leaves.

Pie making was a regular duty in the Dickinson Homestead, and Emily shared in the responsibility. Pies, both sweet and savory, were incredibly popular during Emily's time. Just about anything could be covered in flaky pastry, even the pesky mushroom.

---

6 tablespoons (84 g) unsalted butter
1 ½ pounds (680 g) sliced cremini mushrooms
1 shallot, diced
½ teaspoon dried thyme
¼ cup (30 g) all-purpose flour
1 ½ cups (360 g) mushroom or vegetable broth
2 tablespoons (30 ml) milk
Kosher salt and black pepper
1 sheet frozen puff pastry, thawed

1. Preheat the oven to 400°F (200°C, or gas mark 6).

2. In a large nonstick skillet, melt the butter over medium heat. Stir in the mushroom, shallot, and thyme and cook for 12 minutes, or until the vegetables are softened and the moisture has evaporated. Stir in the flour and cook for 1 minute. Whisk in the broth and bring to a boil. Cook for 2 minutes, or until slightly thickened. Take off the heat. Stir in the milk and season with salt and pepper.

3. Pour the mushroom filling into an 8-inch (20 cm) square baking dish. Top with the sheet of puff pastry and cut a few slits to vent.

4. Place the pie on a rimmed baking sheet and bake for 30 minutes, or until the crust is golden brown and the filling is bubbling. Allow to cool for 10 minutes before serving.

MAKES ONE 9-INCH (23 CM) PIE

Spiced Chicken Wings

Would you like summer? Taste of ours.
Spices? Buy here!
Ill! We have berries, for the parching!
Weary! Furloughs of down!
Perplexed! Estates of violet –
trouble ne'er looked on!
Captive! We bring reprieve of roses!
Fainting! Flasks of air!
Even for Death – a fairy medicine.
But, which is it, sir?

EMILY WROTE THIS POEM, in 1863, in a letter to Samuel Bowles, who was sick at the time. The poem, riddled with metaphors, is an attempt to prove to him the value of her work. Spices represent the healing power of her poems. Her words are a cure, a way to breathe life into one's soul.

When Sue was sick in the summer of 1854, Emily recorded that after feeling much better, Sue ate "a chicken leg" and "desires eating a wing tomorrow." What exactly was in those wings? Unsure. But they sound delicious. And Sue must have thought so too if she helped herself to back-to-back servings.

Chicken wings didn't exist in Victorian America like we know them today. But based on these two accounts, it's safe to say Emily would probably have been a fan.

These crispy oven-baked wings are wrapped in a smoky, spicy dry rub. If you need to tone down the heat, leave out the cayenne pepper. Either way, this dish will clear your sinuses and lift your spirits!

1 ½ teaspoons smoked paprika
1 ½ teaspoons chili powder
1 teaspoon kosher salt
½ teaspoon garlic powder
¼ teaspoon dried oregano
⅛ teaspoon cayenne pepper
2 pounds (910 g) chicken wings

1. Preheat the oven to 425°F (220°C, or gas mark 7). Line a rimmed baking sheet with aluminum foil and place a heatproof wire rack on top.

2. In a small bowl, stir together the smoked paprika, chili powder, salt, garlic powder, dried oregano, and cayenne pepper.

3. Pat the chicken wings dry with paper towels and place them in a large bowl. Sprinkle with the spice mixture and toss to coat.

4. Arrange the wings on the prepared baking sheet. Bake, turning the wings halfway through, for 30 minutes, or until well browned.

MAKES 2 TO 4 SERVINGS

Apple Chestnut Stuffing

"We reckon your coming by the fruit. When the grape gets by, and the pippin and the chestnut — when the days are a little short by the clock, and a little long by the want — when the sky has new red gowns, and a purple bonnet . . ."
—*Emily (1862)*

THE VISUAL IMAGERY in Emily's writing is not just limited to her poetry. Her letters, crafted with care, held the same poetic appeal, stirring and beautiful.

Chestnuts were a popular flavor choice for early American stuffing. In the nineteenth century, the chestnut was basically a complimentary food item. New England housed millions of chestnut trees that sprinkled the ground below with a blanket of sweet and savory nuts.

Pippin was a common type of apple during Emily's life, but any variety will work in its place. Rich chestnuts and fresh apples team up in this old-fashioned stuffing that pairs beautifully with chicken or turkey.

6 tablespoons (84 g) unsalted butter
1 small Gala apple, peeled, cored, and diced
1 small onion, diced
1 rib celery, diced
One 5.2-ounce (145 g) package whole roasted and peeled
 chestnuts, coarsely chopped
1 teaspoon kosher salt
⅛ teaspoon black pepper
1 pound (455 g) dry bread cubes
1 cup (240 ml) chicken broth

1. Preheat the oven to 350°F (180°C, or gas mark 4). Grease a 13 x 9-inch (33 x 23 cm) baking dish.

2. In a large pot, melt the butter over medium heat. Stir in the apple, onion, and celery and cook for 10 minutes, until tender. Take off the heat.

3. Stir in the chestnuts, salt, and pepper. Stir in the dry bread cubes. Pour in the chicken broth and toss to coat.

4. Pour the bread mixture into the prepared baking dish and cover with aluminum foil. Bake for 25 minutes. Remove the foil and continue to bake for 10 minutes, or until golden brown.

MAKES 6 TO 8 SERVINGS

Creamy Green Bean Fricassee

Like Rain it sounded till it curved
And then I knew 'twas Wind—
It walked as wet as any Wave
But swept as dry as sand—
When it had pushed itself away
To some remotest Plain
A coming as of Hosts was heard
That was indeed the Rain—
It filled the Wells, it pleased the Pools
It warbled in the Road—
It pulled the spigot from the Hills
And let the Floods abroad—
It loosened acres, lifted seas
The sites of Centres stirred
Then like Elijah rode away
Upon a Wheel of Cloud.

"THE BEANS we fricasseed and they made a savory cream in cooking," wrote Emily in a letter to her cousins, on a stormy day in May. The rain blew and fell hard from the sky. And Emily missed the company of the birds, who were tucked away in their shelter of trees. In addition to praise for creamy green beans, the poet also included a delicate pressed insect in her correspondence.

Tender green beans are simmered in a rich creamy sauce for a savory side dish that can complement any meal.

20 ounces (560 g) frozen cut green beans
2 tablespoons (28 g) unsalted butter
1 clove garlic, minced
¾ cup (180 ml) heavy cream
Kosher salt and black pepper

1. Cook the green beans according to the package directions. Drain well and set aside.

2. In a large skillet over medium-low heat, melt the butter. Stir in the garlic and cook until fragrant, about 10 seconds. Stir in the green beans and heavy cream. Bring to a simmer. Cook for 3 minutes, or until almost all of the cream is absorbed. Season with salt and pepper.

MAKES 4 SERVINGS

275

Like Rain it sounded till
it curved
~~smelled~~ we
And then I knew 'twas Wind—
It walked as wet as any
Wave
But swept as dry as Sand—
When it had pushed itself
away
to some remotest Plain
A coming as of Hosts was
heard
that was indeed the Rain.
It filled the Wells, it
blazed the Pools
It warbled in the Road—
It pulled the spigot from
the Hills
And let the Floods abroad—
It loosened acres, lifted
seas
the sites of Centres
stirred
then like Elijah rode
away
Upon a Wheel of Cloud.

Pan-Fried Cod Cakes

'Twas such a little, little boat
That toddled down the bay!
'Twas such a gallant, gallant sea
That beckoned it away!

'Twas such a greedy, greedy wave
That licked it from the coast;
Nor ever guessed the stately sails
My little craft was lost!

EMILY USES A BOAT as a metaphor for
the soul in several of her poems. This poem
is essentially about a lost soul. The little boat
was lured out to sea and, though sticking
close to the safety of the shore, was capsized
by a wave. But no one noticed. For Emily, the
greedy wave that enticed her away from safety
could represent many things, like her passion
for poetry or a romantic infatuation.

The sea was an obvious inspiration for
Emily. During her lifetime, the cod fishing
business was booming in the Northeast. Crafty
New Englanders made use of their prized fish
in endless ways. Cod premiered in fish cakes,
boiled dinners, soups, and breakfast hash. By
the end of the century, Boston fisheries were
selling boneless cod and prepared cod cakes.
In a letter to her brother, Emily wrote: "Well,
Austin, dear Austin, you have got back again,
cod fish and pork and all."

These golden fish cakes are well seasoned
and pan-fried until crisp. Don't forget the
tartar sauce!

1 pound (455 g) cooked cod
1 cup (100 g) panko breadcrumbs
2 eggs, beaten
2 teaspoons (6 g) seafood seasoning
3 tablespoons (45 ml) vegetable oil

1. In a large bowl, stir together the cod, breadcrumbs, eggs, and
seafood seasoning until the fish is shredded and the mixture is
combined. Shape into 8 cakes, about ¼ cup (60 g) each.

2. In a large skillet, heat the oil over medium-high heat.
Working in batches, fry the cod cakes for 3 minutes on each
side, or until golden.

MAKES 8 COD CAKES

CHAPTER 5

Emily's BEST Breads

Maggie's Irish
Soda Bread
page 83

Rye and Indian Loaf

Success is counted sweetest
By those who ne'er succeed.
To comprehend a nectar
Requires sorest need.

Not one of all the purple host
Who took the flag to-day
Can tell the definition,
So clear, of victory,

As he, defeated, dying,
On whose forbidden ear
The distant strains of triumph
Break, agonized and clear!

AT FOURTEEN years old, Emily wrote to a friend: "I am going to learn to make bread to-morrow. So you may imagine me with my sleeves rolled up, mixing flour, milk, salaratus [sic], etc., with a great deal of grace."

Emily gracefully continued to perfect her bread baking skills with much success. Her Rye and Indian Loaf took home second place at the Amherst Cattle Show in 1856. Maybe it was hours of practice or an eye for perfection. Or maybe it was the fact that her sister, Vinnie, was sitting on the panel of judges that year.

Rye and Indian Loaf is dense and sturdy and best served with plenty of butter. This round award-winning loaf is slightly sweetened with molasses and bakes up beautifully without a pan.

2 ¼ cups (270 g) whole wheat flour, divided
1 cup (120 g) rye flour
1 cup (140 g) cornmeal
2 teaspoons (10 g) kosher salt
One 0.25-ounce (7 g) package instant yeast
1 ½ cups (360 ml) water
¼ cup (85 g) molasses

1. Line a rimmed baking sheet with parchment paper.

2. In a large bowl, stir together 2 cups (240 g) of the whole wheat flour, rye flour, cornmeal, salt, and yeast. Pour in the water and molasses and stir with a wooden spoon until combined. Knead the dough in the bowl, adding up to ¼ cup (30 g) more whole wheat flour, until a smooth ball forms. It should still be a little sticky.

3. Place the dough on the prepared baking sheet and shape into a 7-inch (18 cm) round. Loosely cover with plastic wrap and lay a towel over the top. Allow the dough to rise in a warm place for 1 hour 30 minutes, or until the dough has expanded to about 10 inches (25 cm) wide and has small cracks on the sides.

4. Meanwhile, preheat the oven to 400°F (200°C, or gas mark 6).

5. When the dough has finished rising, uncover and score a + on the top of the dough with a sharp knife.

6. Bake for 40 to 45 minutes, or until the bread is browned and produces a hollow sound when thumped. Allow to cool before slicing.

MAKES 1 LOAF

Graham Bread

URBAN LIFE in Victorian America was a different world. Big cities were filled with commercial bakers and homemade bread wasn't as common. Health reformer Sylvester Graham, who lived in nearby Northampton, promoted the use of coarse-ground flour and slammed the concept of buying bread. Graham was no physician, but he believed and preached (he actually was a minister) that bread should be made by housewives to ensure its wholesomeness.

In this poem, Emily questions whether heaven is a doctor or a bank. Heaven does not heal in this life, only after death. In exchange for a lifetime of kindness, heaven will reimburse you with a place there. But again, only after death. This was not something Emily signed up for.

This graham bread isn't necessarily a symbol of health, but it was much enjoyed by Emily and her family. The poet wrote to a friend: "Mother heard F-- telling Vinnie about her graham bread. She would like to taste it." This tasty loaf is nutty and toasty and has a hearty texture.

1 cup (120 g) graham flour
1 cup (120 g) all-purpose flour
½ cup (112 g) packed brown sugar
1 teaspoon baking soda
½ teaspoon kosher salt
1 ¼ cups (300 ml) buttermilk
¼ cup (85 g) molasses

1. Preheat the oven to 350°F (180°C, or gas mark 4). Grease a 9 x 5-inch (23 x 13 cm) loaf pan and line with parchment paper.

2. In a large bowl, stir together the graham flour, all-purpose flour, brown sugar, baking soda, and salt. Stir in the buttermilk and molasses just until combined.

3. Pour the batter into the prepared pan. Bake for 1 hour, or until a wooden toothpick inserted into the center of the loaf comes out clean. Cool in the pan for 20 minutes, then unmold and allow the cake to cool on a wire rack.

MAKES 1 LOAF

❧ Gingerbread ❧

The body grows outside, —
The more convenient way, —
That if the spirit like to hide,
Its temple stands alway

Ajar, secure, inviting;
It never did betray
The soul that asked its shelter
In timid honesty.

IN HER MID-TWENTIES, Emily started to pull back from very ordinary social settings. As her anxiety worsened, she gained the status of a recluse. She still continued to give out her delicious treats, but kept her distance. While carefully hiding herself, the cloistered author famously lowered a basket of oval gingerbread from her second-story window for neighborhood children to enjoy.

In this poem, Emily acknowledges the body as an external physical thing. There is a whole world within and the body's main purpose is to house the soul. The body is a temple and it's a place to go if the soul wishes to hide.

These little muffins, inspired by Emily's own recipe, are softly spiced with ginger and sweetened with sticky molasses.

---

3 cups (360 g) all-purpose flour
1 tablespoon (8 g) ground ginger
½ teaspoon baking soda
½ teaspoon kosher salt
½ cup (1 stick, or 112 g) unsalted butter, melted
1 cup (340 g) molasses
½ cup (120 ml) hot water
½ cup (120 ml) heavy cream
1 egg

1. Preheat the oven to 350°F (180°C, or gas mark 4). Line a three 6-well muffin tins with paper liners.

2. In a large bowl, stir together the flour, ginger, baking soda, and salt.

3. In a medium bowl, stir together the melted butter, molasses, hot water, heavy cream, and egg. Pour into the flour mixture and stir just until combined. Pour the batter into the prepared muffin tins, about 3 tablespoons (45 g) in each liner.

4. Bake for 15 to 20 minutes, or until a wooden toothpick inserted into the center of each muffin comes out clean. Cool in the muffin tins for 10 minutes. Remove the muffins to a wire rack and cool completely.

MAKES 18 MUFFINS

Brown Bread

I had been hungry all the years;
My noon had come, to dine;
I, trembling, drew the table near,
And touched the curious wine.

'Twas this on tables I had seen,
When turning, hungry, lone,
I looked in windows, for the wealth
I could not hope to own.

I did not know the ample bread,
'Twas so unlike the crumb
The birds and I had often shared
In Nature's dining-room.

The plenty hurt me, 'twas so new, —
Myself felt ill and odd,
As berry of a mountain bush
Transplanted to the road.

Nor was I hungry; so I found
That hunger was a way
Of persons outside windows,
The entering takes away.

BROWN BREAD WAS ENJOYED by the Dickinson family in all hours of the day, from morning to afternoon. Emily wrote in a letter to her brother: "We had new brown bread for tea – when it came smoking on and we sat around the table, how I did wish a slice could be reserved for you!"

Brown bread is a spin-off of Rye and Indian Loaf (page 72) that came about in New England in the nineteenth century. Made with sour milk and baking soda, and steamed in a tin pudding mold, this new brown bread was loved for its soft and moist texture.

Hunger, in this poem, could represent a variety of desires, such as fame or wealth. But for someone who is used to crumbs, a whole loaf could be overwhelming, even painful.

This recipe uses a technique that allows you to steam in the oven rather than a water-filled kettle. The results are incredibly similar! Enjoy this tender, cake-like bread at breakfast or with a cup of tea or coffee.

---

1 cup (120 g) all-purpose flour
1 cup (120 g) whole wheat flour
¾ teaspoon baking soda
1 teaspoon kosher salt
1 ¼ cups (300 ml) buttermilk
½ cup (85 g) molasses
½ cup (75 g) raisins

1. Preheat the oven to 325°F (170°C, or gas mark 3). Grease a 9 x 5-inch (23 x 13 cm) loaf pan and line with parchment paper. Grease a sheet of aluminum foil.

2. In a large bowl, stir together the all-purpose flour, whole wheat flour, baking soda, and salt. Stir in the buttermilk and molasses just until combined. Stir in the raisins.

3. Pour the batter into the prepared loaf pan. Cover the pan tightly with the aluminum foil, greased-side down, adjusting so there is a hollow dome for the bread to rise.

4. Bake for 1 hour, or until a wooden toothpick inserted into the center of the cake comes out clean. Cool in the pan for 20 minutes, then unmold and allow the loaf to cool on a wire rack.

MAKES 1 LOAF

Twin Loaves

As children bid the guest good-night,
And then reluctant turn,
My flowers raise their pretty lips,
Then put their nightgowns on.

As children caper when they wake,
Merry that it is morn,
My flowers from a hundred cribs
Will peep, and prance again.

EMILY ADMIRED her talent for baking bread. In a letter, she wrote: "Twin loaves of bread have just been born into the world under auspices, -- fine children, the image of their mother; and here, my dear friend, is the glory." The poet humorously personifies two loaves of bread as her fine children, practically a portrait of their mother (aka herself). They are her pride and joy. Her glory.

Bread wasn't the only thing Emily cared for like her own children. Flowers, too, were her offspring. The flowers in this poem are preparing for bed with the same unwillingness as small children when company is at the house. Emily, it seems, was a mother to many things.

It's not known what type of bread these twins were. But this recipe bakes two glorious loaves of soft and fluffy sandwich bread.

5 ⅓ cups (640 g) all-purpose flour
Two 0.25-ounce (7 g) packages instant yeast
1 tablespoon (12 g) sugar
1 ½ teaspoons kosher salt
2 cups (480 ml) water
¼ cup (60 ml) vegetable oil, plus more for brushing

1. In a large bowl, stir together the flour, yeast, sugar, and salt. Stir in the water and oil.

2. Knead the dough on a floured surface for 10 minutes, or until smooth. It should still be a little sticky. Grease the same large bowl and place the kneaded dough in the center. Cover with plastic wrap and allow to rise in a warm place for 30 minutes, or until twice the size.

3. Press the dough down to deflate. Divide the dough in half and shape into two oblong loaves. Grease two 9 x 5-inch (23 x 13 cm) loaf pans. Place the shaped dough into the prepared pans and brush the tops with oil. Loosely cover with plastic wrap. Allow the dough to rise in a warm place for 30 minutes, or until twice the size.

4. Preheat the oven to 400°F (200°C, or gas mark 6).

5. Bake for 30 minutes, or until the loaves are browned and produce a hollow sound when thumped. Place the pans on a wire rack and cover with a towel for 10 minutes to soften the crust. Uncover and allow to cool completely before slicing.

MAKES 2 LOAVES

Little Dinner Rolls

"A new rule is a chance. The bread resulted charmingly, and such pretty little proportions . . . Mother and Vinnie think it the nicest they have ever known, and Maggie so extols it." —*Emily (1882)*

LIKE ANY CURIOUS AND CONFIDENT COOK, Emily was exhilarated by trying out new rules (meaning, recipes). Based on the flood of positive reactions, it seemed that this one was quite a triumph. Emily's letter doesn't specify what type of bread or what ingredients were included, but there's nothing more charming than perfect little dinner rolls, soft and buttery.

2 cups (240 g) all-purpose flour
1 tablespoon (12 g) sugar
One 0.25-ounce (7 g) package instant yeast
1 teaspoon kosher salt
¾ cup (180 ml) water
3 tablespoons (42 g) unsalted butter, melted

1. In a large bowl, stir together the flour, sugar, yeast, and salt. Pour in the water and melted butter. Stir until a dough forms.

2. Knead the dough on a floured surface for 8 minutes, or until smooth. Grease the same large bowl and place the kneaded dough in the center. Cover with plastic wrap and allow the dough to rise in a warm place for 1 hour, or until twice the size.

3. Grease a 9-inch (23 cm) round baking pan. Press the dough down to deflate. Divide and shape into 12 balls. Arrange the shaped dough in the prepared baking pan. Loosely cover with plastic wrap. Allow the dough to rise in a warm place for 30 minutes, or until twice the size.

4. Preheat the oven to 375°F (190°C, gas mark 5).

5. Bake for 15 to 20 minutes, or until the rolls are browned and puffed. Let cool in the pan on a wire rack.

MAKES 12 SERVINGS

Corn Cakes

Morning – is the place for Dew –
Corn – is made at Noon –
After dinner light – for flowers –
Dukes – for setting sun!

ONLY A HANDFUL of Emily's recipe survive today, and Corn Cakes are part of this small collection. Emily enjoyed watching the corn grow and wrote numerous poems about it. She didn't travel much, so nature was her adventure. She met the dew in the morning, watched the corn ripen in the afternoon, and admired the blooming flowers after dinner.

Nineteenth-century cookbooks were flooded with cornbread recipes, so it's no surprise that Emily had a version of her very own. These little Corn Cakes, inspired by Emily's recipe, are made with cornmeal and a touch of whole wheat flour and baked until soft, crumbly, and tender.

1 cup (140 g) cornmeal
1 cup (120 g) all-purpose flour
2 tablespoons (16 g) whole wheat flour
2 tablespoons (24 g) brown sugar
1 tablespoon (8 g) baking powder
1 teaspoon kosher salt
1 cup (240 ml) milk
4 tablespoons (56 g) unsalted butter, melted
1 egg, beaten

1. Preheat the oven to 400°F (200°C, or gas mark 6). Grease an 8-inch (20 cm) square cake pan and cover the bottom with parchment paper.

2. In a large bowl, stir together the cornmeal, all-purpose flour, whole wheat flour, brown sugar, baking powder, and salt. Stir in the milk, melted butter, and egg just until combined.

3. Pour the batter into the prepared baking pan. Bake for 20 minutes, or until a wooden toothpick inserted into the center of the cake comes out clean. Cool in the pan on a wire rack. Slice into 16 squares and serve.

MAKES 16 SERVINGS

Maggie's Irish Soda Bread

The leaves, like women, interchange
Sagacious confidence;
Somewhat of nods, and somewhat of
Portentous inference,

The parties in both cases
Enjoining secrecy, —
Inviolable compact
To notoriety.

MANY SERVANTS WHO WORKED at the Dickinson Homestead were Irish immigrants, who were not seen or treated as equals at the time. But Maggie was a lot more to Emily than just the family maid. She was the poet's kitchen companion, confidante, and friend. Together they washed dishes, baked bread, and snickered about Vinnie's circle of cats.

When Emily turned into a recluse, a rain of hostile judgment came down around her and the town jumped at any opportunity to whisper about the crazy poet. Emily, the mad woman dressed in white, and Maggie, the untrustworthy Irish maid, were a pair of outcasts. In this poem, Emily compares the sound of crinkling leaves to that of whispering, gossiping women.

Irish soda bread, originating in Ireland, became a staple of the Irish daily diet in the nineteenth century. This fluffy, currant-studded bread is probably something Maggie made once or twice at the Dickinson home.

---

2 ½ cups (300 g) all-purpose flour
¼ cup (50 g) sugar
1 teaspoon baking soda
1 teaspoon baking powder
¼ teaspoon kosher salt
4 tablespoons (56 g) unsalted butter, cut into small pieces
½ cup (75 g) currants
1 cup (240 ml) buttermilk

1. Preheat the oven to 375°F (190°C, gas mark 5). Line a rimmed baking sheet with parchment paper.

2. In a large bowl, stir together the flour, sugar, baking soda, baking powder, and salt. Cut in the butter with a pastry blender. Stir in the currants. Pour in the buttermilk and stir until a dough forms.

3. Knead the dough on a floured surface for 2 minutes, or until smooth. Shape the dough into a 7-inch (18 cm) round loaf and place in the center of the prepared baking sheet. Score a + on top of the dough with a sharp knife.

4. Bake for 40 minutes, or until golden and a wooden toothpick inserted into the center of the bread comes out clean. Cool in the pan on a wire rack.

MAKES 1 LOAF

CHAPTER 6

Cakes, Pies
AND OTHER
Sweet Things

Mrs. Dickinson's
Custard Pie
page 99

Black Cake

When roses cease to bloom, dear,
And violets are done,
When bumble-bees in solemn flight
Have passed beyond the sun,

The hand that paused to gather
Upon this summer's day
Will idle lie, in Auburn, —
Then take my flower, pray!

IN HER EARLY FIFTIES, Emily sent her friend, Nellie, a beautiful flower arrangement and her Black Cake recipe, which has survived today.

Victorian America was dazzled by color. Black cake, silver cake, and golden cake were among the era's vibrant bouquet of desserts. In Emily's time, a proper party table would include squares of sliced black cake, and the most elegant parties might showcase an entire black cake center stage.

The poet's recipe called for 2 pounds (910 g) of flour, 5 pounds (2.3 kg) of raisins, and 19 eggs! Though this version is scaled down, it still maintains the intense richness Emily enjoyed so much.

1 ¼ cups (150 g) all-purpose flour
1 teaspoon ground cinnamon
½ teaspoon ground allspice
½ teaspoon ground nutmeg
½ teaspoon kosher salt
½ teaspoon baking soda
1 cup (2 sticks, or 225 g) unsalted butter, softened
1 cup (200 g) sugar
½ cup (170 g) molasses
4 eggs
½ cup (120 ml) brandy
1 pound (455 g) raisins

1. Preheat the oven to 350°F (180°C, or gas mark 4). Grease a 9-inch (23 cm) square baking pan and cover the bottom with parchment paper.

2. In a medium bowl, stir together the flour, cinnamon, allspice, nutmeg, salt, and baking soda.

3. In a large bowl, beat the butter and sugar with an electric hand mixer until fluffy. Beat in the molasses. Beat in the eggs one at a time. Add half of the flour mixture and beat on low speed just until combined. Pour in the brandy and beat on low speed. Add the remaining flour mixture and beat on low speed just until combined. Stir in the raisins.

4. Pour the batter into the prepared pan. Bake for 1 hour, or until a wooden toothpick inserted into the center of the cake comes out clean. Cool in the pan for 20 minutes. Invert onto a wire rack and allow the cake to cool completely.

MAKES 16 SERVINGS

❧ *Coconut Cake* ❧

"I waited to try the cake." —*Emily*

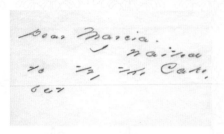

COCONUT, it seems, was a favorite flavor of the poet. Only a handful of recipes from Emily's collection survive today, and two of them feature the tropical ingredient, which the Dickinsons were known to purchase at the town's general store.

Emily's handwritten recipe for Coconut Cake is leavened with baking soda and cream of tartar. She included no instructions for baking the cake but it appears to be a very simple quick bread.

This adapted version is flavored with both shredded coconut and coconut extract and bakes into a golden, moist loaf cake.

2 cups (240 g) all-purpose flour
1 teaspoon cream of tartar
½ teaspoon baking soda
¼ teaspoon kosher salt
½ cup (1 stick, or 112 g) unsalted butter, softened
1 ¼ cups (250 g) sugar
2 eggs
½ cup (120 ml) milk
1 teaspoon coconut extract
1 cup (80 g) sweetened shredded coconut

1. Preheat the oven to 325°F (170°C, or gas mark 3). Grease a 9 x 5-inch (23 x 13 cm) loaf pan and line with parchment paper.

2. In a medium bowl, stir together the flour, cream of tartar, baking soda, and salt.

3. In a large bowl, beat the butter and sugar with an electric hand mixer until fluffy. Beat in the eggs one at a time. Pour in the milk and coconut extract and beat until smooth. Add the flour mixture and beat on low speed just until combined. Stir in the shredded coconut.

4. Spoon the batter into the prepared loaf pan. Bake for 1 hour 15 minutes, or until a wooden toothpick inserted into the center of the cake comes out clean. Cool in the pan for 20 minutes, then unmold and allow the cake to cool on a wire rack.

MAKES 8 SERVINGS

Federal Cake

My country need not change her gown,
Her triple suit as sweet
As when 'twas cut at Lexington,
And first pronounced "a fit."

Great Britain disapproves "the stars;"
Disparagement discreet, --
There's something in their attitude
That taunts her bayonet.

AROUND 1880, Emily sent a parcel of Federal Cake and roses to a friend. Colonial Americans were faithful to England and followed their cookbooks. This eventually changed as Americans identified the need to establish their own style of cooking. Cookbooks featuring American ingredients first appeared around 1800. Foods like Federal Cake, Election Cake, and Independence Cake were a way to insert patriotism into the newly formed American cuisine.

It's speculated that this poem, along with a homemade American flag, was given to Sue on Independence Day. This rich and flavorful cake, spiked with brandy and dried fruit, is perfect for any patriotic holiday.

2 cups (240 g) all-purpose flour
½ teaspoon baking soda
½ teaspoon ground nutmeg
¼ teaspoon kosher salt
½ cup (1 stick, or 112 g) unsalted butter, softened
1 cup (200 g) sugar
2 eggs
½ cup (120 g) sour cream
2 tablespoons (30 ml) brandy
1 cup (150 g) raisins

1. Preheat the oven to 325°F (170°C, or gas mark 3). Grease a 9 x 5-inch (23 x 13 cm) loaf pan and line with parchment paper.

2. In a medium bowl, stir together the flour, baking soda, nutmeg, and salt.

3. In a large bowl, beat the butter and sugar with an electric hand mixer until fluffy. Beat in the eggs one at a time. Beat in the sour cream and brandy. Add the flour mixture and beat on low speed just until combined. Stir in the raisins.

4. Spoon the batter into the prepared pan. Bake for 1 hour 25 minutes, or until golden and a wooden toothpick inserted into the center of the cake comes out clean. Cool in the pan for 20 minutes, then unmold and allow the cake to cool on a wire rack.

MAKES 8 SERVINGS

Coconut Cookies

The Things that never can come back, are several —
Childhood — some forms of Hope — the Dead —
But Joys — like Men — may sometimes make a Journey —
And still abide —
We do not mourn for Traveler, or Sailor,
Their Routes are fair —
But think enlarged of all that they will tell us
Returning here —
"Here!" There are typic "Heres" —
Foretold Locations —
The Spirit does not stand —
Himself — at whatsoever Fathom
His Native Land —

EMILY'S RECIPE for Coconut Cookies has no recipe title, no instructions, and no leavening. It's possible it could even be a sort of cake. Penciled at the bottom of the ingredient list is "Mrs. Carmichael's." Maybe the poet gathered the recipe information from Mrs. Carmichael, who was a friend and neighbor in Amherst. On the back of the coconut recipe is the poem above. It's almost poetic that her two great loves—cooking and writing—share the same page.

These cookies won't spread much while baking, but they are sweet, chewy, and simple enough to make whenever you're craving a sugary treat.

½ cup (1 stick, or 112 g)
   unsalted butter, softened
½ cup (100 g) sugar
1 egg
1 teaspoon coconut extract
1 ¼ cups (150 g) all-purpose flour
½ cup sweetened coconut flakes
½ teaspoon kosher salt

1. Preheat the oven to 350°F (180°C, or gas mark 4). Line two baking sheets with parchment paper.

2. In a large bowl, beat the butter and sugar with an electric hand mixer until fluffy. Beat in the egg and coconut extract. Add the flour, coconut, and salt and beat on low speed just until combined. Wrap the dough in plastic wrap and flatten into a disk. Refrigerate for a minimum of 1 hour.

3. On a lightly floured surface, roll out the dough to ⅛ inch (3 mm) thick between floured parchment paper. Stamp out 2-inch (5 cm) rounds with a cookie cutter. Arrange on the prepared baking sheets. Gather the scraps and roll out more cookies.

4. Bake for 15 to 18 minutes, or until lightly golden around the edges. Allow to cool for 5 minutes on the baking sheets. Transfer the cookies to a wire rack and cool completely.

MAKES ABOUT 3 DOZEN COOKIES

Chocolate Caramels

"I enclose Love's 'remainder biscuit,' somewhat scorched perhaps in baking, but 'Love's oven is warm.'" —*Emily (1877)*

EMILY WAS well versed in the kitchen and cooked everything from a wide assortment of baked goods to breakfast dishes. But the poet was also quite the confectioner, skilled in candy making. Emily was known to send neatly packaged boxes of her rich chocolate caramels, along with the recipe, to her friends and family. The poet sent a parcel of her famous chewy candies with the note above. Apparently, that batch was "somewhat scorched" but I'm sure no one minded.

Many recipes for chocolate caramels in nineteenth-century cookbooks included molasses in the mixture. The recipe here is somewhat of a cross between caramel and chocolate fudge. It's decadent, creamy, and rich. The recipe makes enough to share with friends and they really do make a beautiful gift box.

2 cups (400 g) sugar
½ cup (120 ml) heavy cream
⅓ cup (110 g) molasses
2 ounces (56 g) unsweetened baking chocolate, finely chopped
4 tablespoons (56 g) unsalted butter, cut into pieces

1. Line an 8-inch (20 cm) square baking pan with aluminum foil and grease the foil.

2. In a medium saucepan, bring the sugar, cream, molasses, and chocolate to a boil. Cook, stirring regularly, until the mixture reaches 234°F (112°C) on a candy thermometer. Take off the heat and stir in the butter. Continue to stir vigorously for 5 minutes.

3. Pour the mixture into the prepared pan and allow to cool completely. Slice into 64 portions.

MAKES 64 CANDIES

Maple Sugar Loaf Cake

Presentiment is that long shadow on the lawn
Indicative that suns go down;
The notice to the startled grass
That darkness is about to pass.

THIS POEM EVOKES a sense of foreboding. Inevitably, something harmful is about to happen.

Two years before her death, Emily wrote to her cousins: "Eight Saturday noons ago, I was making a loaf of cake with Maggie, when I saw a great darkness coming and knew no more until late at night." The poet had collapsed on the kitchen floor and her health declined thereafter.

What type of cake Emily was baking when this darkness overtook her is not known. But maple sugar, popular in the nineteenth century, was a sweet ingredient known to be purchased by the Dickinson family. Emily's sister, Vinnie, once "sent [their] father a box of maple sugar" that "she got at the box store."

We can almost be certain that the poet used the amber-hued sugar in some of her bakes. And it's this special sugar, which has notes of caramel, that gives this loaf cake a complex flavor and sweetness.

---

2 cups (240 g) all-purpose flour
½ teaspoon baking soda
¼ teaspoon kosher salt
½ cup (1 stick, or 112 g) unsalted butter, softened
1 cup (200 g) maple sugar
2 eggs
½ cup (120 ml) milk

1. Preheat the oven to 325°F (170°C, or gas mark 3). Grease a 9 x 5-inch (23 x 13 cm) loaf pan and line with parchment paper.

2. In a medium bowl, stir together the flour, baking soda, and salt.

3. In a large bowl, beat the butter and maple sugar with an electric hand mixer until fluffy. Beat in the eggs one at a time. Add half of the flour mixture and beat on low speed. Pour in the milk and beat on low speed. Add the remaining flour mixture and beat on low speed just until combined.

4. Spoon the batter into the prepared pan. Bake for 1 hour 15 minutes, or until a wooden toothpick inserted into the center of the cake comes out clean. Cool in the pan for 20 minutes, then unmold and allow the cake to cool on a wire rack.

MAKES 8 SERVINGS

Cream Puffs

I hide myself within my flower,
That wearing on your breast,
You, unsuspecting, wear me too —
And angels know the rest.

I hide myself within my flower,
That, fading from your vase,
You, unsuspecting, feel for me
Almost a loneliness.

IN THIS POEM, Emily reveals two sides of herself, one that is internal and one that is external. The flower symbolizes feminine beauty and this exterior can hide Emily's private self. When the flower fades, it will be tossed from the vase, along with its concealed consciousness. The person who does this will feel the loss greatly, not only from the flower, but from Emily too.

Emily hid in her real life as well. From her second-story bedroom, carefully concealing herself behind the window covering, Emily lowered a cream puff from a string to a lucky recipient below. Maybe it was her mother who taught the poet how to prepare the sweet delicacy. Mrs. Dickinson was, after all, an expert on crullers. And cream puffs and crullers are both made with French choux pastry.

Each delicate golden puff is filled with fluffy cream and drizzled in warm chocolate sauce.

½ cup (120 ml) whole milk
4 tablespoons (56 g) unsalted butter, cut into pieces
½ cup (60 g) all-purpose flour
Pinch of kosher salt
2 eggs
Whipped cream, for serving
Warm chocolate sauce, for serving

1. Preheat the oven to 400°F (200°C, or gas mark 6). Line a rimmed baking sheet with parchment paper.

2. In a medium saucepan, heat the milk and butter over medium heat until the butter is melted and the mixture is steaming. Add the flour and salt and mix well with a wooden spoon. Continue to cook, stirring vigorously, until the dough forms into a smooth ball. Take off the heat and allow to cool for 5 minutes.

3. Beat in the eggs and continue to beat until the dough is thick but smooth. Drop 12 mounds (2 teaspoons each) of the dough onto the prepared baking sheet.

4. Bake for 15 minutes, then lower the oven to 350°F (180°C, or gas mark 4). Continue to bake for 12 minutes, or until golden brown. Transfer the cream puffs to a wire rack and allow to cool completely.

5. Slice the cream puffs in half horizontally and fill with whipped cream. Drizzle with warm chocolate sauce.

MAKES 12 CREAM PUFFS

Mrs. Dickinson's Custard Pie

Remorse is memory awake,
Her companies astir, —
A presence of departed acts
At window and at door.

It's past set down before the soul,
And lighted with a match,
Perusal to facilitate
Of its condensed despatch.

Remorse is cureless, — the disease
Not even God can heal;
For 'tis his institution, —
The complement of hell.

MRS. DICKINSON was well known for her marvelous custards. Like Emily, Mrs. Dickinson found joy in cooking for those she loved. Once, when Austin didn't show up for a special dinner their mother had prepared with her son in mind, and Emily felt it was her duty to inform him just how hurtful and inconsiderate his absence was. This poem explains that remorse can awaken the memory to indecent past acts. In scolding Austin, Emily was trying to conjure guilt in her brother. It's hard not to smile at this display of affection for her family.

This creamy pie, flavored with fresh lemon and vanilla, is definitely something you don't want to miss.

3 egg yolks
One 14-ounce (392 g) can sweetened condensed milk
Zest and juice of 2 lemons
1 teaspoon vanilla extract
1 store-bought graham cracker crust
Whipped cream, for serving

1. Preheat the oven to 325°F (170°C, or gas mark 3).

2. In a large bowl, beat the egg yolks. Whisk in the sweetened condensed milk, lemon juice and zest, and vanilla.

3. Place the crust on a rimmed baking sheet and pour the filling into the crust. Bake for 25 minutes, or until the filling is set. Allow to cool to room temperature.

4. Refrigerate for a minimum of 3 hours, or until chilled. Serve with whipped cream.

MAKES 8 SERVINGS

Cinnamon Doughnuts

"The lovely flower you sent me is like a little vase of spice, and fills the hall with cinnamon." —*Emily (1885)*

EMILY ADMIRED DOUGHNUTS. The poet wrote down a recipe for the beloved pastry and penciled "Kate's doughnuts" on the back. Nutmeg is the only spice in Kate's doughnuts, but the recipe below pairs the fragrant spice with woodsy cinnamon. These baked yeast doughnuts are soft and tender and will fill your house with a wonderful sweet and spicy aroma.

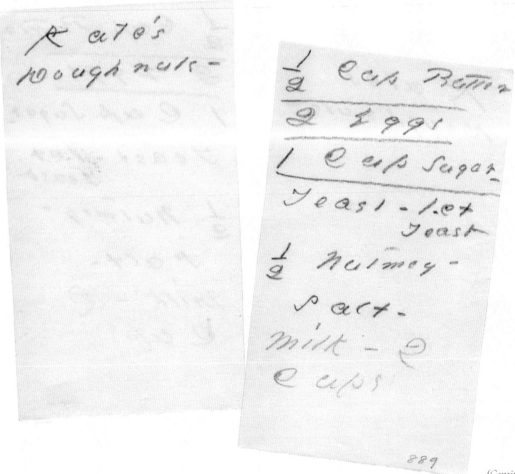

(Continued)

DOUGHNUTS

3 ¼ cups (390 g) all-purpose flour

⅓ cup (65 g) sugar

One 0.25-ounce (7 g) package instant yeast

1 teaspoon ground cinnamon

1 teaspoon kosher salt

¼ teaspoon ground nutmeg

1 cup (240 ml) milk

4 tablespoons (56 g) unsalted butter, melted

1 egg

TOPPING

½ cup (100 g) sugar

½ teaspoon ground cinnamon

4 tablespoons (56 g) unsalted butter, melted

1. To make the doughnuts, in a large bowl, stir together the flour, sugar, yeast, cinnamon, salt, and nutmeg.

2. In a medium bowl, whisk together the milk, butter, and egg. Pour the milk mixture into the bowl with the flour and stir until a shaggy dough develops. Knead the dough on a floured work surface for about 8 minutes, or until smooth.

3. Grease the large bowl and place the dough in the center. Cover with plastic wrap and allow to rise in a warm place for 1 hour 30 minutes, or until twice the size.

4. Line two rimmed baking sheets with parchment paper. Press the dough down to deflate and roll out on a floured surface to ½ inch (12 mm) thick. Using a 3-inch (7.5 cm) round cutter, stamp out rounds of dough. Using a 1-inch (2.5 cm) round cutter, stamp out a hole in the center of each round. Arrange on the prepared baking sheets. Loosely cover with plastic wrap and allow to rise in a warm place for 30 minutes, or until nearly twice the size.

5. Preheat the oven to 350°F (180°C, or gas mark 4).

6. Bake the doughnuts for 14 minutes, or until the internal temperature of the doughnuts is 190°F (88°C). Allow to cool for 5 minutes.

7. To make the topping, whisk together the sugar and cinnamon in a small bowl. Dip the tops of the doughnuts in the melted butter, then dip in the cinnamon sugar.

MAKES 1 DOZEN DOUGHNUTS

Chocolate Mousse

"**PEOPLE MUST** have puddings," Emily said to friend and correspondent (and possible love interest) Thomas Wentworth Higginson.

A nineteenth-century radical, Thomas was a vocal abolitionist and women's rights proponent who advocated his beliefs in a cultural magazine called *The Atlantic Monthly*, which is still published today. Amidst the Civil War, Thomas published an advice piece for those aiming for a byline. Emily responded with four tender poems and a scribbled note, which hit him with the seductive one-liner, "Are you too deeply occupied to say if my Verse is alive?" Thomas was entranced, and thus began a quarter-century-long correspondence between the two.

Emily didn't literally mean pudding when she made that comment to Thomas. *Pudding* was once an umbrella term for dessert. But Emily actually did have a recipe for something quite like the literal version and sent it to her neighbor in 1872.

This silky chocolate mousse is luscious and sweet and definitely a must-have.

1 cup (165 g) semisweet chocolate chips
½ teaspoon instant espresso powder
Pinch of kosher salt
1 ½ cups (360 ml) cold heavy cream, divided
½ teaspoon vanilla extract
Chocolate shavings, for garnish

1. In a medium bowl, stir together the chocolate chips, espresso powder, and salt.

2. In a small saucepan, heat ½ cup (120 ml) of the cream over medium heat until steaming.

3. Pour the warm cream over the chocolate and allow to sit for 5 minutes. Add the vanilla and stir until smooth. Allow to cool for 10 minutes, stirring periodically.

4. In a medium bowl, add the remaining 1 cup (240 ml) cream and beat with an electric hand mixer until soft peaks develop. Transfer ½ cup (120 ml) of the whipped cream to a small bowl; set aside in the refrigerator. Continue beating the remaining whipped cream until stiff peaks form.

5. Add a third of the whipped cream to the cooled chocolate mixture and fold with a rubber spatula. Fold in the remaining whipped cream in two additions.

6. Scoop the mousse into four small serving dishes and refrigerate for a minimum of 2 hours.

7. Dollop with the reserved whipped cream and garnish with chocolate shavings before serving.

MAKES 4 SERVINGS

Notes on Sources

EGG-IN-A-BASKET WITH CHIVES
- "happy egg and toast provided by Maggie"
  - Dickinson, E. (2012). *Letters of Emily Dickinson*. New York: Dover Publications.

SPICY SKILLET HASH
- Poem: Will there really be a morning?
  - Public-Domain-Poetry.com

SHEET PAN SAUSAGE BREAKFAST
- Poem: Morning that comes but once
  - Amherst College Digital Collection
- "meat and potato"
  - Dickinson, E., and T. V. W. Ward. (1986). *The Letters of Emily Dickinson*. Cambridge, MA: Belknap Press of Harvard University Press.

STRAWBERRY OATMEAL
- Poem: Forbidden fruit a flavor has
  - Amherst College Digital Collection

GLAZED CRULLERS
- Poem: She sweeps with many-colored brooms
  - AmericanLiterature.com
- "crullers and custard"
  - Sewall, R. B. (1994). The Life of Emily Dickinson. Cambridge, MA: Harvard University Press.

STICKY BAKED PEACHES
- Poem: Talk not to me of Summer Trees
  - Amherst College Digital Collection

BAKED BERRY PECAN FRENCH TOAST
- Poem: The morns are meeker than they were
  - AmericanLiterature.com
  - Public-Domain-Poetry.com

APPLE PANCAKES
- Poem: A drop fell on the apple tree
  - Poets.org
- "Our apples are ripening fast. I am fully convinced that with your approbation they will not only pick themselves, but arrange one another in baskets and present themselves to be eaten."
  - Dickinson, E. (2012). *Letters of Emily Dickinson*. New York: Dover Publications.

JASMINE TEA BISCUITS
- Poem: Come slowly, Eden!
  - AmericanLiterature.com

RICE CAKES
- Poem: The grave my little cottage is
  - Amherst College Digital Collections

HONEY LEMONADE
- Poem: The pedigree of honey
  - Amherst Digital Collection
- "there were many little dances, with cake and lemonade at the end"
  - Dickinson, E. (2012). *Letters of Emily Dickinson*. New York: Dover Publications.

HAM AND CUCUMBER TEA SANDWICHES
- Poem: If anybody's friend be dead
  - Public-Domain-Poetry.com
- "Oh, I will see you again at the Dickinson tea party"
  - Bianchi, M. D., and E. Dickinson. (1971). *The Life and Letters of Emily Dickinson*. New York: Biblo and Tannen.

RASPBERRY JAM
- Poem: She rose to his requirement
  - Public-Domain-Poetry.com

CHERRY SCONES

• "I wish you could have some cherries – if there was any way we would send you a basket of them – they are very large and delicious, and are just ripening now."
  ◦ Dickinson, E. (2012). *Letters of Emily Dickinson.* New York: Dover Publications.
• "Today is very beautiful – just as bright, just as blue, just as green and as white and as crimson as the cherry trees full in bloom."
  ◦ Dickinson, E. (2012). *Letters of Emily Dickinson.* New York: Dover Publications.

WINTER GARDEN VEGETABLE SOUP

• Poem: A little Snow was here and there
  ◦ Amherst College Digital Collection

BEEF BONE BROTH

• Poem: There's something quieter than sleep
  ◦ Amherst College Digital Collections
• "flown"
  ◦ Dickinson, E., and T. V. W. Ward. (1986). *The Letters of Emily Dickinson.* Cambridge, MA: Belknap Press of Harvard University Press.

BROTHY CHICKEN SOUP

• "had eaten chicken broth twice"
  ◦ Dickinson, E., and T. V. W. Ward. (1986). *The Letters of Emily Dickinson.* Cambridge, MA: Belknap Press of Harvard University Press.

SUE'S OYSTER STEW

• Poem: We outgrow love like other things
  ◦ Amherst College Digital Collections

PUMPKIN CORN CHOWDER

• Poem: 'Twas just this time, last year, I died
  ◦ Amherst College Digital Collections

IRISH STEW

• "Maggie is making a flying visit to cattle-show, on her very robust wings—for Maggie is getting corpulent."
  ◦ Dickinson, E. (2012). *Letters of Emily Dickinson.* New York: Dover Publications.

LEMON HERB CHICKEN

• Poem: Before I got my eye put out
  ◦ Public-Domain-Poetry.com
• "For the first few weeks I did nothing but comfort my plants . . . I chop the chicken centres when we have roast fowl."
  ◦ Dickinson, E. (2012). *Letters of Emily Dickinson.* New York: Dover Publications.

VEGETARIAN NIÇOISE SALAD

• "The garden is amazing – we have beets and beans, splendid potatoes."
  ◦ Dickinson, E. (2012). *Letters of Emily Dickinson.* New York: Dover Publications.

VEAL MEATBALLS WITH GRAVY

• Poem: Some keep the Sabbath going to church
  ◦ Public-Domain-Poetry.com
• "Isn't that a dinner fit to set before a King."
  ◦ Dickinson, E. (2012). *Letters of Emily Dickinson.* New York: Dover Publications.

MUSHROOM POT PIE

• Poem: The mushroom is the elf of plants
  ◦ Amherst College Digital Collection

SPICED CHICKEN WINGS

• Poem: Would you like summer?
  ◦ Dickinson, E. (2012). *Letters of Emily Dickinson.* New York: Dover Publications.
• "a chicken leg"
  ◦ Dickinson, E., and T. V. W. Ward. (1986). *The Letters of Emily Dickinson.* Cambridge, MA: Belknap Press of Harvard University Press.
• "designs eating a wing tomorrow"
  ◦ Dickinson, E., and T. V. W. Ward. (1986). *The Letters of Emily Dickinson.* Cambridge, MA: Belknap Press of Harvard University Press.

APPLE CHESTNUT STUFFING

• "We reckon your coming by the fruit. When the grape gets by, and the pippin and the chestnut – when the days are a little short by the clock, and a little long by the want – when the sky has new red gowns, and a purple bonnet – "
  ◦ Dickinson, E. (2012). *Letters of Emily Dickinson.* New York: Dover Publications.

CREAMY GREEN BEAN FRICASSEE

- Poem: Like Rain it sounded till it curved
  - Amherst College Digital Collection
- "The beans we fricasseed and they made a savory cream in cooking"
  - Dickinson, E. (2012). *Letters of Emily Dickinson.* New York: Dover Publications.

PAN-FRIED COD CAKES

- Poem: 'Twas such a little, little boat
  - Public-Domain-Poetry.com
- "Well, Austin, dear Austin, you have got back again, codfish and pork and all"
  - Dickinson, E. (2012). *Letters of Emily Dickinson.* New York: Dover Publications.

RYE AND INDIAN LOAF

- Poem: Success is counted sweetest
  - AmericanLiterature.com
  - Public-Domain-Poetry.com
- "I am going to learn to make bread to-morrow. So you may imagine me with my sleeves rolled up, mixing flour, milk, salaratus, etc., with a great deal of grace."
  - Dickinson, E. (2012). *Letters of Emily Dickinson.* New York: Dover Publications.

GRAHAM BREAD

- Poem: Is Heaven a physician?
  - Amherst College Digital Collection
  - Public-Domain-Poetry.com
- "Mother heard F-- telling Vinnie about her graham bread. She would like to taste it."
  - Dickinson, E. (2012). *Letters of Emily Dickinson.* New York: Dover Publications.

GINGERBREAD

- Poem: The body grows outside
  - Public-Domain-Poetry.com

BROWN BREAD

- Poem: I had been hungry all the years
  - Public-Domain-Poetry.com
- "We had new brown bread for tea – when it came smoking on and we sat around the table, how I did wish a slice could be reserved for you!"
  - Dickinson, E. (2012). *Letters of Emily Dickinson.* New York: Dover Publications.

TWIN LOAVES

- Poem: As children bid the guest good-night
  - Public-Domain-Poetry.com
- "Twin loaves of bread have just been born into the world under auspices, -- fine children, the image of their mother; and here, my dear friend, is the glory"
  - Dickinson, E. (2012). *Letters of Emily Dickinson.* New York: Dover Publications.

CORN CAKES

- Poem: Morning – is the place for Dew
  - Amherst College Digital Collections
  - Public-Domain-Poetry.com

LITTLE DINNER ROLLS

- "A new rule is a chance. The bread resulted charmingly, and such pretty little proportions . . . Mother and Vinnie think it the nicest they have ever known, and Maggie so extols it."
  - Dickinson, E. (2012). *Letters of Emily Dickinson.* New York: Dover Publications.

MAGGIE'S IRISH SODA BREAD

- Poem: The leaves, like women, interchange
  - Public-Domain-Poetry.com

BLACK CAKE

- Poem: When roses cease to bloom, dear
  - Amherst College Digital Collections
  - AmericanLiterature.com

COCONUT CAKE

- "I waited to try the cake"
  - Amherst College Digital Collection

FEDERAL CAKE
- Poem: My country need not change her gown
  - Public-Domain-Poetry.com

COCONUT COOKIES
- Poem: The Things that never can come back, are several
  - Amherst College Digital Collection

CHOCOLATE CARAMELS
- "I enclose Love's 'remainder biscuit,' somewhat scorched perhaps in baking, but 'Love's oven is warm.'"
  - Dickinson, E. (2012). *Letters of Emily Dickinson.* New York: Dover Publications.

MAPLE SUGAR LOAF CAKE
- Poem: Presentiment is that long shadow on the lawn
  - Public-Domain-Poetry.com
- "Eight Saturday noons ago, I was making a loaf of cake with Maggie, when I saw a great darkness coming and knew no more until late at night."
  - Dickinson, E. (2012). *Letters of Emily Dickinson.* New York: Dover Publications.
- "You know Vinnie sent father a box of maple sugar – she got at the box store"
  - Dickinson, E. (2012). *Letters of Emily Dickinson.* New York: Dover Publications.

CREAM PUFFS
- Poem: I hide myself within my flower
  - Amherst College Digital Collection

MRS. DICKINSON'S CUSTARD PIE
- Poem: Remorse is memory awake
  - Public-Domain-Poetry.com

CINNAMON DOUGHNUTS
- "The lovely flower you sent me is like a little vase of spice, and fills the hall with cinnamon."
  - Dickinson, E. (2012). *Letters of Emily Dickinson.* New York: Dover Publications.
- "bang the spice"
  - Dickinson, E. (2012). *Letters of Emily Dickinson.* New York: Dover Publications.

CHOCOLATE MOUSSE
- "people must have puddings"
  - Dickinson, E., and T. V. W. Ward. (1986). *The Letters of Emily Dickinson.* Cambridge, MA: Belknap Press of Harvard University Press.
- "Are you too deeply occupied to say if my Verse is alive?"
  - Dickinson, E. (2012). *Letters of Emily Dickinson.* New York: Dover Publications.

INTERLUDE
- "a prickly art"
  - Dickinson, E. (2012). *Letters of Emily Dickinson.* New York: Dover Publications.
- "head-quarters"
  - Dickinson, E. (2012). *Letters of Emily Dickinson.* New York: Dover Publications.

Acknowledgments

A MILLION THANKS TO MY AGENT, Sharon Bowers. Your advice, support, and humor keep me going. And for that, I am incredibly grateful. This project wouldn't have been possible without you.

Thanks also to Dan Rosenberg, my editor at Quarto, for the opportunity to write this book. I have adored every minute of it.

About the Author

ARLYN OSBORNE is a graduate of the French Culinary Institute in New York City. Her work can be found on The Food Network, The Kitchn, Food52, Serious Eats, *Bon Appetit*, and *The Washington Post*.

Index

NOTE: Page references in *italics* indicate photographs.